A
River
Seen
Right

Also by Michael Baughman:

MOHAWK BLOOD

A River Seen Right

Michael Baughman

Photographs by J. Daniel Callahan

LYONS & BURFORD
PUBLISHERS

Copyright © 1995 by Michael Baughman

All photographs © Dan Callaghan

All Rights Reserved. No part of this book may be reproduced in any manner without the express written consent of the publisher, except in the case of brief excerpts in critical reviews and articles. All inquiries should be addressed to: Lyons & Burford, Publishers, 31 West 21 Street, New York, NY 10010.

Printed in the United States of America

10 9 8 7 6 5 4 3 2 1

Baughman, Mike.
  A river seen right / Michael Baughman.
    p. cm.
  ISBN 1-55821-421-6 (cloth)
    1. Fly fishing — Oregon — Umpqua River — Anecdotes. 2.
Steelhead (Fish) — Oregon — Umpqua River. 3. Trout — Oregon
— Umpqua River. 4. Baughman, Mike. I. Title.
  SH539.B38 1995
  799.1'2'0979529 — dc20   95-19198
                                                            CIP

For my grandson Billy Hansen, age two:

MAY HEALTHY RIVERS AND WILD FISH
BE A PART OF HIS FUTURE.

CONTENTS

North Umpqua

Rock Creek

Canton Creek

Williams Cr.

CAMP WATER

Fall Cr.

Fairview Cr.

Bogus Cr.

Archie Cr.

STEAMBO INN

MOORE'S LOG HOUSE

N. Umpqua River

Cowgay Cr.

Wright Cr.

Fox Cr.

```
0   1   2   3   4   5   6   7   8   9   10  11  12  13  14  15
└───┴───┴───┴───┴───┴───┴───┴───┴───┴───┴───┴───┴───┴───┴───┘
      S c a l e        i n         M i l e s
```

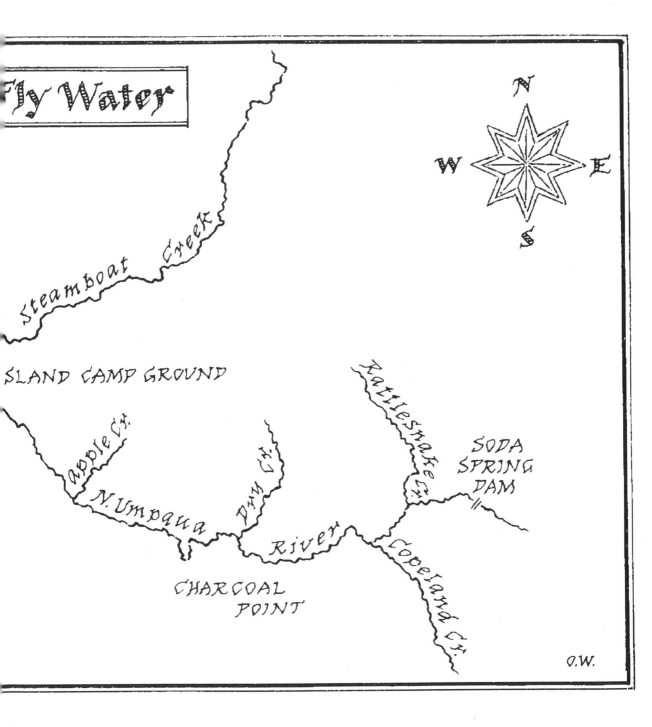

Lower end of Big Island

1

Good Beginnings

*One river, seen right, may well be all rivers
that flow to the seas.*

JOHN GRAVES
Goodbye to a River

I MOVED TO ASHLAND, OREGON, in the summer of 1966 with my wife
Hilde and our young son Pete. There were many reasons for the move, among
them the offer of a good job. But far more important to me was the fact that
southern Oregon is famed for its many excellent rivers. As a boy of five or six,
I had begun learning to catch trout on a good creek that ran through my
great-grandfather's farm in western Pennsylvania. From there I went on to

Hawaii, Colorado, Florida, Germany, California, and everywhere I went I fished, in rivers, lakes, and oceans, and did it with a strong passion. The Northwest, I was sure, would allow that passion to develop further; and during our first fall and winter, I caught both resident trout and steelhead on the fly in the Rogue, Klamath, Applegate, and Illinois rivers. They were lovely streams and exciting fish, and I knew I'd come to the right place for sure.

Fishing those streams, talking to other anglers I met there, I heard a lot about the North Umpqua. It was the prettiest river on earth, some said, and challenging, too, with more than thirty miles of the upper river restricted to fly fishing only. Summer-run steelhead arrived there early—at the latest, by the Fourth of July—and they were big, bright, wild fish. I also heard about Frank Moore who, with his wife Jeanne, ran the Steamboat Inn at the very heart of the fly water. He was the one to talk to about finding and catching fish.

So I made the three-hour drive north from Ashland in mid-June because I didn't feel I could make myself wait until July.

This river and country were everything I'd heard about and hoped for, even more: Douglas firs and sugar pines the size of mature redwood trees; clear, cold blue-green water; boulder-strewn pools; churning whitewater rapids ("umpqua" meant "thunder water" in the local Indians' language); smooth, deep runs over black bedrock ledges and clean white gravel; thickly forested canyon walls with steep rock cliffs; and fish. I remember feeling the presence of steelhead even as I saw that water for the first time driving by.

I quickly set up my tent at Island Campground, about a mile above the confluence with Steamboat Creek, and then drove down to Steamboat Inn, just below the creek. It was early afternoon, bright and hot; probably the worst time of day to catch a steelhead on a fly, but I wasn't going to waste time waiting for sunset.

Frank Moore wasn't at the inn, but I met and talked to his wife Jeanne, who was kind and helpful even to an ignorant stranger. She told me that her husband was in Roseburg for the day, and that the most popular fishing spots were found on the quarter-mile or so of river between Steamboat Creek and the inn—called the Camp Water, I would soon learn—and that a few early steelhead had been taken through that week.

I fished hard until dark, and my initiation to the North Umpqua was similar to what many anglers have gone through before and since. My felt wader soles, perfectly fine in all the other places I'd fished, didn't hold very well on the slick bedrock ledges, and as a result I fell in three or four times. My eight-foot rod and double-tapered line, all I'd ever needed on the Rogue or Klamath, couldn't get my Skunk fly out to many of the best-looking places. I hooked a few nice rainbow trout, but never got a touch from a steelhead.

It had been a very enjoyable day, though, and back at the campground, which I had to myself, I was happy eating a can of fairly cold stew with a can of fairly warm beer and watching bats and nighthawks swooping and darting out over the dark, rushing water.

I finished a breakfast of instant oatmeal and coffee well before light the next morning, then drove back downstream and parked across the Mott Bridge near Steamboat Creek and fished my way down the trail along the south bank, trying every likely looking spot along the way. Eight hours later, I was back at the car, fishless again (and soaked again, too), and tired enough to head back to camp for a sandwich and a couple of hours of rest.

At about four in the afternoon, I tried the Steamboat Inn again. This time Jeanne told me that Frank was out on the river, trying out a new rod with a guest.

Then, on the short drive back up to the Mott Bridge from the inn, I finally saw him. I was sure who it was at once, and I parked along the road to watch. Two fishermen in chest waders were standing on a shallow ledge at the top of a pool that I would later learn is called the Upper Kitchen. The one doing the casting, a short, powerfully built man, had to be Frank.

I'd watched a fair number of people casting flies, in many places over many months, but I'd never seen anything like this. At first he was handling sixty or seventy feet of line, laying it out flat and straight with a single backcast. Soon it was eighty feet, then ninety, then a hundred, then more. It appeared to be virtually effortless, and if someone had photographed the two dozen or more casts I watched, then superimposed the photos one upon the others, it would have appeared as a single picture—except for the lengths of the casts. I was very impressed. In fact, I felt intimidated because I knew I was watching something that, no matter how long I worked at it or how hard I tried, I would never be able to do myself. Most of us have had that same sensation at some time or other, when we see somebody who is thoroughly, even magically gifted at something we happen to care about. But more than anything else it was a beautiful thing to see, and I watched until Frank and his guest began wading back out of the river.

That evening, just before dark, after a total of eighteen or twenty hours of wading and casting, I finally hooked my first North Umpqua steelhead. It was near the top end of the Lower Boat Pool, which, for a newcomer, is some of the most obvious-looking holding water on the river. I was knee-deep on a ledge with fifty or sixty feet of floating line out and the Skunk fly within an instant of stopping at the end of its slow swing. The strike was sudden, heavy, violent. Before I could react, the fish was far out of water, a writhing silver female in the fading evening light. She was gone downstream after the jump, running out the rest of my line and at least fifty yards of backing before she jumped again and again, bright against the dark water. Luckily, that is one of the easiest places on the river to follow a fish. Five minutes later, down near the Kitchen Pool, I slid her over clean gravel into shallow water. The very best summer steelhead are the native fish that come in June, thick and bright from the sea and with enough stored energy to last them through the winter to their spawning. This was one of them, and though it weighed only seven pounds, it made me as happy as any fish I'd ever caught anywhere. It certainly attached me to the North Umpqua, firmly and forever.

The next morning—I went fishless again, but really didn't mind it—I finally found Frank Moore at the inn. When he had finished cooking breakfasts for some guests, we drank coffee and sat and talked at the long, eight-inch-thick sugar-pine table in the dining room, and the friendship that began then—the first of many friendships that began on the river— has lasted nearly thirty years.

Hilde and I spent the summers of 1971 and 1972 working for the Moores at the inn. I fished every day and, with Frank's guidance, began to really understand the North Umpqua. Those were wonderful summers with good runs of fish. Hilde hooked her first one in the Kitchen Pool in 1971, and since then has probably caught more North Umpqua steelhead than any woman in the river's history (the largest so far, a bright native male, measured just over a yard long). Our son Pete's first fish came in 1972, from the Station Pool. He was ten years old, and the smallest waders we could find to buy him reached to his neck. Ingrid, only five in 1972, waited until she had grown into the same waders to begin her angling life with a wild twelve-pounder from the Ledges.

So I'm now into my fourth decade of fishing and learning the North Umpqua, which is a good portion of anyone's life but a very insignificant span of time nonetheless. For tens of thousands of years before any humans arrived, earthquakes and volcanic eruptions formed and re-formed the Cascade Mountains. Trickles of melted ice and snow became seasonal streams, then perennial creeks, plunging and winding their clear, cold way down through the heavy timber to the river. The steelhead and salmon ran and spawned, ran and spawned.

Indians established campsites on the banks along Steamboat Creek as long as six thousand years ago and probably hunted the country and fished the creek, as well as the main river, well into the nineteenth century. In my own brief time, I've seen wild-looking hippies rattling up Highway 138 in their brightly painted vans and ancient buses, seeking places to "live off the land," and then rattling back down, usually after the year's first rain; the boom and bust of logging, and the sudden importance and subsequent hatred, by many, of northern spotted owls; the waxing and waning of environmentalism; commercial ocean-fishing bans; Indian treaty-rights controversies; the vogue of fly angling, and the resulting arrival of wealthy sportsmen in shiny four-wheel-drives, wearing tailored waders and casting weighted flies with indicators on thousand-dollar graphite rods.

Much of what has happened to the North Umpqua, and many of those who have come to it and keep coming, cause real concern for the river's future. (This is just as true, of course, for hundreds of other coastal streams.) But, at least for now, the snow melts and the creeks cut down the mountainsides, and the North Umpqua fish keep running. Some of us love these simple rhythms as much as we love anything, and this book is my attempt, with Dan Callaghan's inestimable help, to explain that love through showing you the river.

Sawtooth Pool with Mott Bridge in the background

2

Sneaking Down to the Water

And this our life, exempt from public haunt,
Finds tongues in trees, books in the running brooks,
Sermons in stones, and good in every thing.

SHAKESPEARE
As You Like It, Act II, Scene 1

FLY FISHING gives us a lot of time to think and remember, and there is much about the North Umpqua—all other fine rivers too, I'm sure—that can channel thoughts and memories in interesting directions.

Two years ago, I began my season in early June, as I usually do, because this is the best time of year to hook a really spectacular fish. Though considerably diminished over the past twenty years, there is still a run of big natives that moves upriver early to turn up Steamboat Creek, then Canton Creek, and hold there in low water through the summer. These spawning tributaries are quite rightly protected, so hooking a fast-moving early-summer steelhead is mostly a matter of luck and perseverance. But when one is hooked—well, more about that later.

Another good thing about early June is that the river isn't very crowded yet. On the day I remember, I started my morning at the confluence of Steamboat Creek and the river, thinking that, not long after first light, a fish or two might turn up the creek after a night in the Station Pool.

I parked just across the Steamboat bridge and climbed down the short, steep trail to the triangle of land formed where the two streams meet. Though the water was still fairly high—downstream a couple of hundred yards the Kitchen Rock was still well under water—the spring runoff was all but over. Six weeks earlier, the trail I was on had been submerged.

That was why I stopped to examine the tree wells facing upstream. A few minutes of searching will occasionally produce an arrowhead either whole or nearly so, and if not that, at least some chips or fragments that have washed down Steamboat Creek to be trapped by the lowering water.

This was one of my lucky days. Between two big roots at the base of an old fir tree, I found a leaf-shaped point about half buried in damp earth and in perfect shape except for the missing quarter inch of a lower corner. These leaf-shaped points are at least three thousand years old and possibly twice that age. I examined it with my Mini-Mag light and then, after a minute or two, placed it back where it had come from, as I always do.

But I thought about that point as I waded out across the gravel toward the deep creek channel to make a series of cross-stream casts that would cover the likeliest water.

Then, as I made my first short cast, I remembered a story Frank Moore told me about the early run. The first summer after he returned from infantry combat duty in World War II, he had come to the river on June 1, just to look things over, and, from the same bank where I had parked my car, he saw a steelhead roll in the Station Pool. He "happened to have a fly rod along," as he put it, and climbed down to fish. With the Camp Water all to himself, he hooked fifteen steelhead between the Station and the Mott that day; and for the next two weeks, with the river deserted, he made the nearly two-hour drive from Rosenburg to the Camp Water every evening with similar results.

I stripped off a yard of line and cast again, then watched the floating line swing across the Steamboat Creek channel. ("Steamboat" is an old mining term. A "steamboated" miner was one who worked a claim that didn't pan out. There was a significant gold rush in this area in the 1870s, so the name of the creek probably indicates a lack of success and profit.)

Whether it was three thousand years ago or twice that long, the Indians who hunted and fished this country surely knew about the early run of steelhead. They, too, took advantage of the lowering, clearing water at the end of the runoff. No doubt they had their favorite places, learned through generations of trial and error—certain cliffs, certain rocks and gravel bars—where they speared fish from above as they passed through shallow water, or as they turned up the creeks in pods or schools.

And these early fish do sometimes travel together in large groups. I proved that to my own satisfaction twenty years ago, several miles up Canton Creek where there is a large, deep pool with a steep, narrow waterfall at its head. Once the early fish reach this point, they are stopped until the high water of a fall or early winter storm allows their passage over the falls to the creek's upper reaches. For several years in a row, in late July or early August, I hiked up to the big pool with a diving mask and snorkel. I think it was 1975 when I checked the pool with my mask late on the evening of July 31 and didn't find a single steelhead there. Because I was camped not far downstream, I went back the next day, just to enjoy the swimming, and more than eighty big fish had arrived. They must have come early that morning, having moved together across shallow gravel bars downstream that weren't even deep enough to keep them completely submerged.

The local Indians knew about it all, and they used their knowledge. Though they fished with crude equipment, their well-developed skills probably kept them fed adequately through all but the hardest years.

Besides fish, they had deer and elk, grouse and mountain quail, and dozens of edible roots and berries, including the area's prolific camas bulbs; but on June days like this one they most likely went after steelhead. They butchered and smoked most of the fish they speared, but I'm sure they also celebrated by cooking some freshly caught ones over a blazing vine-maple fire. Some fish were eventually pounded into meal and mixed with dried berries and fat to be preserved as pemmican. Fish heads were saved to be used in soup in the winter time, hearts were roasted and eaten immediately, and all bones were put back into the river to ensure that the runs would return again.

One thing I always wonder about: Did they ever fish merely for fun? When they had all the meat they could possibly preserve, when they were too full to eat another bite, did some of the men make excuses to their wives and then sneak from the camp back down to the water to fish some more, simply because of the happiness it gave them? My guess is yes.

It was a good thing I had no pressing need for meat because I didn't find a fish that morning at the confluence.

Light comes quickly in the mornings. Driving downstream from Steamboat Creek, I didn't even need my headlights. What I did need was an answer to the same old question: Where to fish?

North Umpqua steelhead spots can be classified in various ways. There are low-water places and high-water places; dry fly and wet fly; greased line and conventional drift; morning and evening; sunlight and shade.

I heard the log truck behind me, then glanced in the rearview mirror and saw the muddy, dented grill eight or ten feet off my bumper. At Williams Creek—where Zane Grey had one of his camps directly across the river, and where he suffered the first of a series of strokes that eventually killed him—I used the pullout to let the log truck pass, then watched the load of old-growth Douglas fir disappear around a downstream bend.

Indians were still fishing for meat, and probably for fun, a mere hundred years before the serious logging started. Up until the North Umpqua Highway was completed to Steamboat in 1955, relatively little was done to disturb the watershed. By the time Highway 138 reached Diamond Lake in 1964, hundreds of miles of minor roads branched from it, opening up some of the Northwest's last and most magnificent ancient forests.

I've worked in the woods enough to have a respect for those who do it for a living. Felling big trees, setting chokers on steep slopes—all of it is hard and exceedingly dangerous work. Driving the huge trucks along narrow roads, sometimes for fourteen or sixteen hours a day, six or even seven days a week in the busy times, is either insane or courageous. (The driver who passed me at Williams Creek had either left home by 3:00 a.m. or spent the night in his truck in the woods to get an early start in the morning.)

But the results of all of this have been inevitable: Spawning creeks are clogged with debris. In every storm, tons of mud wash from logged off slopes to silt the once-clean gravel. With shade gone, water temperatures rise ten or twenty degrees or more, and trout, salmon, and steelhead die by the millions. Roads are surely the principal curse of rivers.

And I drove the road to Lower Archie—an early-season, high-water pool—to try again.

At Lower Archie it's possible, even in fairly high water, to see fish from the high bank if they hold in either the cross-stream pocket or along the roadside ledge; but nothing was visible today. I climbed down to the high rock we cast from and covered the submerged boulder at midstream first and then the V. On my last cast I had a moment of excitement. Something struck hard just above the break and took out several feet of line, but I knew at once it was only a trout: a native rainbow of sixteen inches that on many streams would have been a trophy but here, on this morning, rated barely above an irritation. (It's strange the way we often diminish our own enjoyment with inflexible expectations.)

After Lower Archie I tried Wright Creek, wading carefully out until the water was within three or four inches of my wader tops. Four mergansers flew upstream in a line, barely off the water, close to the trailside bank. I changed from a Skunk to a Thor and covered all the best water with no sign of a fish. As I waded back out, I heard an osprey whistling shrilly, then saw it soaring high above in the day's first sunlight.

Fairview would be much too high to hold fish, and so would The Gorge, so I drove downstream all the way to Fox Creek. When I passed Rip Rap, a spectacular green cliff with a boulder-strewn pool below it and a steep rapids just downstream, I remembered that not long after the road went in, the California Oregon Power Company (COPCO) had wanted to build a dam at this location. Why? By all accounts I've ever heard, simply because the massive cliffs on both sides of the canyon would have made it an ideal place to build one. Presumably, to a power company, a dam has greater value than thirty-some miles of wild, lovely river and all its abundant life. Luckily, COPCO was finally persuaded to build its dams high on the upper river.

Fox Creek is just far enough off the road so that it doesn't get fished as often as most other equally productive places in the area. It's not quite a pool, but not really a riffle either. Above long and very powerful rapids, the river bends gently and spreads and slows, with a deep pocket about twenty yards above the break, fairly close to the roadside bank. The pocket is the only place I've ever hooked a fish in high June water.

As soon as I reached the end of the trail down from the road and squeezed through the alder trees to the river, I knew that the wading wouldn't be easy. I could probably get far enough out from the alders to roll cast, but that would be all.

Luckily, it was all I needed. On my third cast, with only five or six yards of line out, I got one of those heavy slow-water strikes: The fly stopped and the line tension increased gradually until, after two or three seconds, I felt that immovable and unmistakably living weight out there.

The rod bowed as I raised it, and the steelhead thrashed heavily and wildly on the surface—a male, I could tell, bright and at least ten pounds—and then he ran, straight down with no hesitation, over the break and into the whitewater, gaining speed all the way. By the time I waded back out to the bank, my fly line was out of sight downstream; and when I tried to reel the line tight, I soon knew that the fish was gone. Feeling happy and disappointed at once—which might be possible only in fishing—I reeled all the backing and my line in and saw, as I'd suspected, that the eight-pound tippet had snapped at the fly.

All in all, it had been a fine start to my season.

As I grow older, I love fishing as much as ever—more all the time, in fact—but hooking fish has become less important than it used to be. On the rare summer mornings when steelhead are both plentiful and aggressive, I'm apt to quit at 7:00 a.m. after two or three fish, because anything more than that is wasted on me anyway.

One good fish hooked and lost in early June is plenty, so I drove from Fox Creek back upstream to what Hilde and I call our North Umpqua cabin. Frank Moore owns eighty acres of land between Fairview Creek and Fall Creek, and we rent the place from him. A former homestead, it is a simple house in a quiet clearing by a pond a few hundred yards from the Moores's log house, high above the river on the old dirt road that was once the only way into this country.

Just as I often think of Indians when I fish near the mouth of Steamboat Creek, when we spend time at the cabin, I find myself trying to imagine what life was really like for homesteaders and pioneers. All I can know for certain is that it had to be very hard: hard simply to get here, hard to clear land, to build moderately comfortable dwellings, to secure adequate food and clothing, to raise children, to create any semblance of cultural life. There were fierce storms, devastating droughts, and uncontrollable fires. Illness and untimely death were common.

So Indians came from Asia across to North America with the lowering of the oceans in the Late Pleistocene era, and some eventually worked their way to the North Umpqua. Eventually they were followed by trappers, miners, homesteaders, road builders, loggers, engineers, farmers, ranchers, tourists in their motor homes and, yes, fly fishermen too.

No matter where our allegiances lie, one unarguable fact is always worth remembering: The steelhead were here long before any of us.

3

———

8-F-4

*There is nothing which has yet been
contrived by man by which so much happiness is produced
as by a good tavern or inn.*

JAMES BOSWELL
The Life of Samuel Johnson

WHEN I WALKED through the Steamboat Inn's front door for the first time, nearly thirty years ago, the first thing I noticed (the first thing nearly everybody notices, I'm sure) was the massive sugar-pine table and benches that take up the entire middle of the long dining room. These impressive furnishings have been the centerpiece of Steamboat dining ever since they were built by a logger and a young fishing guide in the 1930s, just as the inn

Steamboat Inn with Jim Van Loan on the roof,
Jack Hemingway on the ground

and its predecessors have been at the hub of the North Umpqua's fly-fishing activity.

But there was another accoutrement of the inn that ended up impressing me even more than that big, glossy table. On the wall behind the counter where rods, reels, lines, and flies were sold was an old-fashioned crank telephone, and its number was 8-F-4. More than anything else, it was this antique—yet functional—phone that made me feel I really was in a virtual wilderness.

I soon learned that it was easier to get a call through from our Ashland home to Hilde's parents in Germany than it was to reach Frank and Jeanne Moore, barely one hundred miles away. Sometimes operators merely laughed and broke the connection when you told them the number you wanted was 8-F-4. And calling out of the inn usually wasn't any easier. Everything had to begin with a Forest Service operator at the ranger station across the river, and if she was busy with somebody else, or having lunch, or maybe even enjoying the view, you waited. When you did get the operator, your call was relayed to the high-voltage power lines to Roseburg, where the telephone company extracted it and routed it to its final destination. Besides all those complications, crank phones can be tricky and subtle, and if this one was mishandled (or was simply in some kind of electronic bad mood) it could loose a mechanical shriek that left me deaf in one ear for half an hour or more. So even when log trucks and motor homes roared by on Highway 138 sixty feet away, and even if men had walked on the moon recently, a place containing such a telephone with 8-F-4 as its number could be considered remote.

To my mind the most amazing (and sometimes most frightening) thing about the twentieth century is how quickly our world changes. Now, barely a quarter century later, the inn conducts its business with the help of the most advanced computers. Power lines have been strung across the roadside mountains, and, on an instant, satellites and transoceanic cables can connect Steamboat Inn with San Francisco or Singapore.

For someone visiting the area for the first time in the 1990s, it might be difficult to visualize what things were like a relatively short time ago.

It wasn't until 1927, the year Babe Ruth hit sixty home runs, that a dirt road reaching as far as Steamboat was finally gouged through the timber and into the steep canyon walls. (An angler fishing the Lower Boat Pool today can see the old road angling down to the river a little ways below Steamboat Creek.)

It was this rough, sometimes treacherous road that allowed the establishment of the first North Umpqua fishing camps. Major Lawrence Mott arrived in 1929, the year of the Great Depression, and put his camp on the south bank, opposite Steamboat Creek. When Mott died at age fifty in 1931, the camp was taken over by an employee named Zeke Allen.

Nineteen thirty-one was also the year that dentist-turned-writer-and-sportsman Zane Grey arrived to fish the North Umpqua for the first time. Although he was without doubt the most famous angler to have visited the river, he definitely wasn't the best liked. Not happy with Allen's accommodations, he established his own more elaborate fishing camps, first near the confluence of Canton and Steamboat creeks (it was still legal to fish in the tributary creeks in those days), then across the main river from Allen's camp, next at Maple Ridge Point at the present site of Steamboat Inn, and finally downstream, across the river from Williams Creek. Grey apparently always traveled with a large entourage, including friends, helpers, cooks, cameramen, and "secretaries," who presumably were there to assist him with his writing projects. Since then, it has been reported that these secretaries actually performed somewhat more basic services. It is also well known that Grey, noted for his competitiveness as an angler, stationed underlings at or even in his favorite pools in the early mornings to reserve them until he arrived ready to fish. Local fishermen didn't take well to this at all, and Grey's egocentric behavior is quite likely the reason that no pools or North Umpqua landmarks bear his name.

In 1934 a southern Californian named Clarence Gordon, who had come to know the North Umpqua through visits on his way to and from fishing expeditions to Canada, was granted Forest Service approval to set up a fishing camp. Located on the south bank—his kitchen tent looked out onto what is now the Kitchen Pool—Gordon's North Umpqua Lodge soon became popular, through his apparently skillful promotion, with well-to-do southern Californians. Like Grey, Gordon had his local detractors: in his case those who resented the presence of these out-of-state, relatively wealthy clients (and there are locals today who continue to harbor similar resentments).

At the urging of the Forest Service, Gordon soon built a permanent lodge with cabins and a small stone cottage for tying flies. In these early years, the accommodations were simple, and much of the food served at the lodge was of very local origin. Harry and Dolly Killeoir, an ex-vaudeville team, cooked for Gordon and, by all accounts, despite the understandable limitations, did it very well.

The war slowed business down in the 1940s. Shortly after the war ended came changes that would dramatically alter the North Umpqua River forever. Nets and fish racks had been reducing anadromous fish runs for years (nets remained in the river until 1949), but this was something even worse, because it would be permanent: a major road, to be built along the river grade (following the old dirt road much of the way), eventually to reach all the way from Roseburg to Diamond Lake. This paved highway provided easy access to both dam builders and timber companies, and results were predictable and quick.

Because of the dam construction upstream near Toketee, river levels fluctuated wildly and erratically, to the detriment of both fishermen and fish runs. Tons of mud and silt are further results of both dam and road building, especially when the road is next to the river.

There was one unarguable benefit of these otherwise unfortunate developments: In 1951 Gordon, along with members of Roseburg hunting and fishing clubs, convinced the State Game Commission that a fly-fishing-only restriction was needed to protect declining numbers of North Umpqua salmon and steelhead. The section of river set aside in the new regulations, from Rock Creek upstream to Soda Springs, is the same lovely thirty miles of fly water we enjoy today. (One change, though, is that in recent years Roseburg hunting and fishing clubs have periodically tried, so far unsuccessfully, to get the fly water, or portions of it, reopened to bait and lures.)

Upstream dam building made conditions so bad that, through most of the early 1950s, the river at Steamboat was unfishable. As a result, the North Umpqua Lodge closed. Gordon did run a store on the north bank near Steamboat Creek during this period, serving mostly construction workers now instead of fishermen, and he claimed that he made more money at that than he had at the lodge—seven thousand dollars worth of hamburgers and beer (mostly beer, sometimes by the truckload) in one summer. Eventually he moved the store to the present location at Steamboat Inn, where he put up the building that still (though remodeled and enlarged extensively) serves as the inn's dining room and kitchen.

I've heard various explanations why Clarence Gordon finally decided to give up his lodge, leave the area forever, and return to southern California. The most logical conclusion would be that he simply became tired of conditions, over which he had no control, affecting his business adversely; but, by the time he left in 1957, things were beginning to look better. With much of the construction completed and its end in sight, the river, though surely changed, would soon return to a semblance of normal. People who knew Gordon say that his wife Delia, a graduate of the Juilliard School of Music, didn't like the area nearly as much as he did. It could simply have been that someone who had known the North Umpqua as lonely and relatively unspoiled didn't care to see what it might become in a more commercial and technological future.

Whatever the reasons, Clarence Gordon's decision to leave became Frank Moore's opportunity. Frank and Jeanne ran a restaurant in Roseburg at the time, and Frank had been fishing the river harder and more successfully than anyone else since returning from the war in Europe in 1946. Old-timers say that his green pickup truck with a canoe on top was seen more often than any other vehicle in the area in those days. When he wasn't fishing for fun, he was guiding for Gordon. After he began working for Gordon, Frank heard rumors that Gordon had hired him primarily to keep him from fishing the river on his own. Whether that was true or not, there is a well-known local story about a classified ad that Jeanne and the hired help, back in the restaurant, ran in the Roseburg paper: *Lost: One owner and manager of Moore's Cafe. Last seen up the North Umpqua River.*

When Gordon decided to sell his store and head south, Frank immediately arranged a loan from Colonel Jim Hayden, a veteran North Umpqua fisherman. Once the deal was completed and the Moores had moved in, Frank began building guest cabins down the hill below the main lodge. While the building was going on, he guided his guests, and also contacted anglers in other areas to assure them that the river and its steelhead fishing were coming into shape again. Meanwhile, Jeanne, under primitive and very difficult conditions, served meals to crews of construction workers and Forest Service employees in the dining room.

Soon the new Steamboat Inn was a successful business, and most of the serious fishermen who came—or came back—returned year after year: Colonel Jim and Laddie Hayden, Court and Betty Decius, Court's son Jack and Anne Decius, Stan and Yvonne Knouse, Dan and Mary Kay Callaghan, Zane's son Loren Grey, Don and Gayle Haines, Ken and Polly Anderson, Norm and Sally Christensen, Dave and Bev Carlson, Art and Dotty Cohen, Bruce and Gloria Duncan, George and Marian Peak, Fred and Margaret Telonicher, Jack and Puck Hemingway, and many others, often with large families. At crowded times there were beds and sleeping bags everywhere—on the porches and lawns, even in the shop. Sometimes the Moore children gave up their own beds to the overflow of guests.

There was a small but fascinating irony at work at Steamboat Inn after the completion of the paved highway. Remember the big sugar-pine table in the dining room, which had been in use since the 1930s, and had been built by a fishing guide and a logger? The making of that impressive piece of furniture was surely one of the very few times in the history of the area that a fisherman and a logger cooperated in anything.

With the highway came multitudes of loggers, and to accommodate them there were first hundreds—then thousands—of miles of dirt and gravel roads branching off the main highway, snaking up through the mountains, reaching into vast stands of trees as big and old and as valuable as any on the continent. From before dawn until after dusk, empty log trucks roared up the road past the inn, and roared back down toward Roseburg mills, loaded with gigantic logs of fir, cedar, and pine.

One result of this was that many of the conversations held around that big old table at the inn had to do with the effects of this logging, and what—if anything—could be done to stop it, or at least slow it down.

Frank Moore was an Oregon native, a great-grandson of early pioneers, and he understood very clearly what the irresponsible cutting of too many trees was doing to the river he loved. Spawning tributaries were clogged with slash. With trees cut to the very banks of the streams, shade was gone and summer water temperatures soared to dangerous levels. During winter storms, mud and silt washed off the clear-cut slopes, and off the dirt roads themselves, down into the creeks and eventually into the main river.

There were two significant responses to all of this. First, in 1966, an organization called the Steamboaters was formed, its stated purpose "to preserve the natural resources of the North Umpqua." The regular guests at the inn formed the nucleus of the group, and they would be joined over the ensuing years by hundreds of anglers and conservationists from many states, and even foreign countries. The club logo was designed by Ken Anderson, art director at Walt Disney Studios at the time. Stan Knouse, a retired geologist, became the first president. Clarence Gordon and Roderick Haig-Brown were named as honorary members, as were Governors Tom McCall and Bob Straub.

Probably the most significant and effective undertaking of The Steamboaters in the 1960s was the making of a short, powerful movie called "Pass Creek" (one of the tributary streams that had been devastated).

In the summer of 1967 two California filmmakers, Hal Riney and Dick Snider, came to the inn to fish. But when Frank sat them down at the sugar-pine table to talk and then took them into the back country and showed them what the loggers had been doing, Riney and Snider made a quick trip back to California and returned to the inn with their camera equipment instead of their fly rods.

Their expertise produced twelve minutes of very persuasive commentary on the situation. "Pass Creek" documented the destruction going on in the Steamboat Creek drainage, but it didn't presume to ask that the logging be stopped; only that it be carried out responsibly: that roads be built sensibly, that spawning tributaries be protected, and that buffer strips of trees be left along banks to provide shade and soil stability.

Frank kept a small plane in Roseburg, and he flew "Pass Creek" anywhere there was an audience willing to watch it. Sometimes it didn't really much matter whether they were willing or not. When a timber company or BLM spokesman made a speech somewhere arguing that more logging as usual was what the country really needed, Frank was often close behind with his movie, to balance things.

I remember Frank's showing "Pass Creek" at an environmental symposium at the college in my hometown of Ashland. In the question period afterward, a professor asked, his ivory-tower academic disapproval clear, why the movie had focused on fly fishing to make its point. Frank's answer—the only possible answer—was that fly fishermen usually study, know, and care more about rivers and the life in them than anybody else.

"Pass Creek" was eventually shown all the way back in Washington, D.C., and proved instrumental in the passage of both state and federal legislation regulating logging practices. Frank was appointed to the Oregon State Game Commission and, with fellow Steamboater Dan Callaghan, served under Governor Tom McCall for many years. The governor visited Steamboat Inn, sang songs around the sugar-pine table, and hooked and landed his first steelhead—a fine eight-pounder—in the Kitchen Pool.

Loggers and governors surely weren't the only people who used Highway 138. As the fame of the North Umpqua grew, the inn and river were visited by ever-increasing numbers of anglers. Roderick Haig-Brown came from British Columbia to fish and snorkel through the Camp Water and, again at the big table, he argued with Frank about whether steelhead feed once they enter fresh water. Haig-Brown said they didn't. A couple of years later, Frank caught a big male steelhead in January, its stomach absolutely stuffed with small black nymphs. He removed the stomach carefully, packed it in dry ice and airmailed it to Haig-Brown who, always the gentleman, wrote back allowing that perhaps steelhead did feed in fresh water from time to time.

It was a period of both increased fishing pressure on the river and increased environmental awareness; a time of sometimes painful transition from the philosophy of cut-and-run to an understanding that rivers and forests and planets have definable limits. Very few anglers took pictures of dead fish anymore. A steelhead caught in the fly water was very apt to be released.

In 1975 Frank sold the inn and moved downstream about five miles to his eighty acres between Fairview Creek and Fall Creek, where he built a two-story log house high above the river on the old road from Roseburg. The new owners, Jim and Sharon Van Loan, began a new era at Steamboat Inn, one that reflects the greatly increased popularity of fly fishing, particularly with upper-income people.

The cabins have been remodeled, and sumptuous suites and housekeeping cottages have been added. While Clarence Gordon relied heavily on venison and steelhead, and Frank and Jeanne were apt to cook steak and potatoes or pork chops for the late fishermen's dinner, a guest today will more likely be served red snapper with jalapeño lime marinade, or Cornish hens with fruited wild-rice stuffing, and walnut praline mousse for dessert. Sharon and inn manager Pat Lee have published their recipes in two literate and popular cookbooks.

Jim Van Loan has served in his turn for many years on the State Fish and Wildlife Commission, and Steamboaters continue their active involvement in all matters relating to hydroelectric dams, road building, and logging. The northern spotted owl—a lovely, inoffensive little creature—has come to symbolize the continuing and often bitter struggles between timber companies, government agencies, and conservationists. Years of Steamboater work went into the eventual designation of the North Umpqua as a Wild and Scenic river.

The sugar-pine table is still there, right where it always was; but the inn's phone number has gone from 8-F-4 all the way to (503) 498-2411.

Black's Pool, angler Dennis Black

4

Summer Questions

To anticipate, not the sunrise and the dawn merely,
but, if possible, Nature herself!

HENRY THOREAU
Walden

IT WOULD BE LOGICAL to conclude that the most important questions about a river that has been fished for more than fifty years by thousands of skillful anglers were answered satisfactorily long ago. But that definitely isn't the case. I've always felt that one of the most appealing things about fishing is the fact that even the apparently simplest problems often have no absolute solutions. Partly this is because of the unpredictability of all natural cycles; partly it's a matter of individual experience and personal taste. The questions I include here are those asked by nearly everyone who visits the North Umpqua; but the answers are only mine, with all of the built-in limitations that fact implies.

When do the summer fish arrive?

Frank Moore really did find the main run all the way up to the Camp Water on June 1 one year. Many old-timers continue to begin their years around the middle of June, give or take a week or so, depending on water conditions and the fish count at Winchester Dam, just east of Roseburg. I always make at least one trip to the river in June, too, and will continue to for as long as I'm able, even though the early run seems to decline year by year.

But if I had to recommend a good time to a friend with limited opportunities, I'd suggest the second week in July without hesitation.

In 1971 Hilde and I began our first summer working at Steamboat Inn on June 15. All six cabins were occupied, with at least one good fisherman in each of them—fishermen who put in at least four hours each morning and another four or so at night before showing up at the fishermen's dinner, which was served at 10:30 p.m. Naturally enough, nothing much other than fishing was discussed at the table, and up until the end of June there weren't more than a dozen steelhead hooked by guests—a group average of less than one per day. Other fishermen were on the river, and, if anything, their luck was even worse. (I worked breakfast with Frank, serving mostly log-truck drivers and logging crews, but I went out every evening to fish from 5:00 until dark, and hooked just two fish in June, one at the Lower Boat Pool and one downstream at Burnham.)

Things improved a little through the first few days of July; not so much because more fish had arrived, but because more people were trying for them. The inn remained booked up, and now the campgrounds were filling, too.

On the evening of July 6, I'd fished down the Mott trail without luck and was walking back to my car in the dark when something told me to wade across to the Station Pool. (Regulations allow fishing until one hour after sunset, so this was perfectly legal.) I waded over carefully, feeling my way across the gravel and through the ledges with both feet and my left hand. By the time I arrived at the ledge at the head of the pool, there weren't more than twenty legal minutes left. In that time I hooked and landed two bright fish, a six-pound male and then a jumping nine-pound female, both of them strong and wild—and because I covered only the top end of the long pool I felt that if time had allowed, there were surely more steelhead to be caught there.

Then, on the morning of July 7, everybody was hooking steelhead. Happy fishermen began coming into the inn at 8:30 or 9:00 for breakfast and, of course, talking about it.

"They're all over the place out there," a doctor from the Bay Area said— a guest who, up until then, had gone almost a week without a strike. "I hooked one in the Upper Boat right at daylight, the first place I fished, on my third or fourth cast. Then, while I played it, some guy came in and hooked another one in the exact same place. Then I hooked another one there! Then he hooked another one there. Then, after we both headed downstream, another guy hooked one there!"

A stranger eating bacon and eggs in his waders at the long table had been listening with a smile. "They're downstream, too!" he said. "I got a couple of good ones at the Tree Pool!"

A log-truck driver drinking coffee joined the conversation. "I saw a guy packing one up to his car down by Wright Creek," he said, "and then somebody had one on upstream a little ways, out on that island."

"Coleman," I said.

"I don't know the names of the pools," the driver answered, "but it looked like a good fish."

"Hell, they're all good," the doctor said.

In 1972, our second working summer at the inn, the first really productive fishing day came on July 11. I've never been one to keep written records of my fishing, but I do have a good memory for the important things in life, and I know that the first large run of fish has arrived between July 5 and July 15 in at least fifteen of the last twenty summers. My long-standing habit is to begin a week or so of fishing the first Monday after the Fourth of July, and I'm seldom disappointed.

What is the best time of day to fish?

I remember reading in one of Haig-Brown's books that, in his opinion, the most productive fishing hours were between ten in the morning and four in the afternoon. There are times when I wish I could believe in this theory, but I can't—certainly not in regard to summer steelhead on the North Umpqua.

One reason some of the best fishing of the summer usually occurs immediately after the fish arrive is that steelhead tend to be most aggressive then, presumably because there is something about a new temporary environment that makes them willing to move to a fly. As a general rule, the longer a fish remains in a pool, the harder it is to catch—perhaps because a migratory fish becomes more comfortable, or less inclined toward irritation or curiosity, as it becomes used to its immediate surroundings.

On the North Umpqua, at any time of year, morning is when you are most apt to find fresh steelhead in a pool; and if you do find them, they are fish that haven't yet seen a fly in that particular location. This is the most convincing reason I can give to explain the fact that, all things such as pools fished and hours spent fishing them being equal, I have caught more than twice as many morning fish as evening fish over the years.

New fish in a pool or not, there are other practical reasons for fishing early on summer mornings. Instead of the eighty- or ninety-degree temperatures you can expect on any July or August evening (which means you have a choice of either wading wet and becoming chilled as darkness falls, or sweating a quart or two into your waders), the first few hours of daylight will always be pleasantly cool. The river has cooled overnight, too, and this can be an important factor from midsummer on, when daytime water temperatures commonly reach well into the sixties. At least as unpleasant as the afternoon heat—and a direct result of it—are the hard winds that gust upstream nearly every summer afternoon and evening. In contrast, mornings are certain to produce a calm that makes casting easier and accurate. Beyond all of this, there is a feeling of freshness, of new possibilities, that comes with the first soft dove gray light of dawn. Whether or not the steelhead you are fishing for have moved overnight, you can be sure they haven't seen a fly, or a sloppy cast, or a raft or kayak, for eight hours or more.

But the best reason of all for getting up in the dark to fish early—the only truly good reason—is because you actually enjoy it, as I do. Since early childhood, I've been a "morning person." When I lived in Hawaii, I got up early to spearfish, even though there were enough good places within reach of an outrigger canoe to accommodate the entire population of spearfishermen on Oahu at once. Hilde and I keep a small boat in Baja and often spend a couple of summer weeks fly-fishing for dorado there. We're always on the water before the edge of the orange sun shows over the Sea of Cortez near Carmen Island, even though we know the best fishing probably won't begin for another two hours. It's simply that we love being out on the ocean before dawn, and we also love being on the river then. To us it is unquestionably the very finest time of any day.

Yet I'm well aware of the fact that many expert fishermen hate getting up early. Rob Carey, one of my oldest North Umpqua friends, hates getting up about as much as anyone I've ever known. Once I made the very stupid mistake of trying to convert him.

This was more than twenty years ago, during an early July when the Upper Kitchen Pool was producing more fish than any other place on the river.

He'd been having a period of bad luck, as we all do, and I wanted to help him break it by getting him into the Upper Kitchen first in the morning. Nothing about accomplishing this was easy: nothing from dragging him out of his sleeping bag, to pouring black coffee down his throat, to lacing up and tying his studded boots, to stuffing him into the passenger seat of my car. But I got him to the ranger station parking lot, and then down the trail in the dark, past the Sawtooth and the Hayden Run, the Upper and Lower Boat, and there we finally were, ahead of anybody else, at the Upper Kitchen.

"Where are we?" Rob asked.

"Right where we want to be," I answered.

"Anybody else around?"

"Maybe somebody was out at the Station. It's too dark to be sure. You ready?"

"For what?"

"To fish."

No answer.

"Let's wade out," I said, and we did.

Luckily, getting out to fish the Upper Kitchen is an easy wade; a gradual descent over gravel in a steady, gentle current.

"You wake enough to fish, Rob?"

"Sure."

"They've been holding all over the place out here. Especially right out in front of the Kitchen Rock and across on the other side of it."

"Sure."

"You all set?"

"Sure."

"Don't cast until I'm out of the way."

"Sure."

I waded out in a hurry, then stood on the gravel bank about ten yards behind Rob to watch. I won't pretend to remember how many casts it took, but I know he hooked a fish before two minutes had passed—a good fish, too. It ran far down into the Kitchen Pool, jumped there, and hit the water with a splat so loud it sounded like a beaver's tail.

A few minutes, two short runs, and three jumps later, Rob had worked his steelhead back upstream and soon had it close enough for release.

Then he hooked a second fish almost immediately. This one jumped at the strike but didn't go far. By the time he had it played out, there was light enough to see another fisherman down in the Mott and one upstream in the Lower Boat.

After his second fish had been released, Rob waded out to join me.

"Nothing to it," I said.

Nothing showed on his face—nothing I could see—and without a word, he started back toward the car.

Fifteen minutes later, I dropped him off back at Island Campground, and as I backed out of our space to head downstream, he was sitting on the picnic table, slowly unlacing his boots.

When I returned sometime between nine and ten, Rob was on the picnic table—not still on it, but back on it—lacing his boots back up, getting ready to go fishing.

"How'd you do?" he asked me.

"I hooked two, but I worked a lot harder for mine than you did."

A quizzical look crossed his face, followed by a faint smile. "You mean I really did get a steelhead this morning?"

"Don't kid me," I said.

"Kid you about what?"

"Are you serious?"

"Serious about what?"

"About the fish you hooked this morning."

He shook his head, still smiling. "I thought I remembered it. But then when I woke up a while ago, I figured maybe it was a dream. But then I saw how wet my boots were, so I wasn't sure. Where'd we go? Some place in the Camp Water?"

"Are you serious?"

"Sure!"

The conversation went around in a few more circles, until Rob had convinced me beyond any doubt that he really didn't quite remember fishing the Upper Kitchen that morning.

So the moral is obvious enough: Why get up if you don't want to? There are places and ways to catch fish all day long.

It's a general rule everywhere that, all things being equal, summer steelhead fishing is best when the water is in shade. Most experienced North Umpqua anglers can tell you within minutes when their favorite pools become sunny in the morning and shady in the evening on the second week in July or the last week in August, or anytime in between.

Most of us also know that there are pools, runs, and riffles in which fish rise fairly well despite bright sunlight. Just a few widely known examples:

Between nine and ten in the morning, the Station Pool is likely to produce a steelhead or two, even though it has already been well fished by as many as half a dozen people.

Just downstream, where Rob Carey landed two fish in his sleep at the Upper Kitchen, around eleven in the morning is a good time to try. (If he had known that at the time, I never would have roused him.)

After the Upper Kitchen, it's worth going down through the Mott.

I've had fish rise at Wright Creek any time of day.

The Famous Pool is the first spot in the fly water coming upstream from Glide, and dozens—probably hundreds—of summer steelhead have been taken there at two or three in the afternoon, under bright sun with the wind howling.

Once the river drops to its true summer level, usually by the middle of July, dry flies are well worth trying; and dry flies are almost always most effective with sun on the water.

If floaters won't produce, a greased line approach with wet flies sometimes will. (My definition of that technique is a lot simpler than Jock Scott's: a natural, drag-free drift of the fly over a fish on a floating line.)

The very best time of all to be fishing on a summer day has nothing to do with the clock, but a little to do with the calendar. Almost every August, and certainly every September, a long hot spell will be broken by a front of low pressure moving in over the mountains from the coast. Sometimes this change of weather is predicted days in advance, but just as often it comes as a surprise—a very pleasant one if you happen to be on the river when it happens. When the temperature drops ten or fifteen degrees—and, even better, when that drop is accompanied by a gentle rain—steelhead that have held on the bottom sullen and immovable for days or weeks will suddenly not merely rise to a fly, but will often chase one across the surface of a pool and strike at it three or four times before they finally manage to hook themselves.

The most convincing anecdote I've ever heard on this subject comes from Dan Callaghan. Many years ago he was fishing the Upper Mott on a warm August afternoon, during a period when very few fish had been hooked anywhere on the river for many days—one of those disheartening stretches when you actually begin to doubt that there are steelhead in the river, or that there ever were or ever will be again. Two of Dan's friends, Stan and Yvonne Knouse, were fishing the Lower Mott just below him, and three other anglers were just upstream, two in the Kitchen and one in the Upper Kitchen.

Very suddenly, within a matter of minutes, some dark, heavy clouds had rolled in. The temperature fell quickly, and minutes later, a cool, light rain began. Within seconds after the first drops hit the water, Dan hooked a fish. By the time he looked downstream, Stan and Yvonne both had fish on. When he glanced back upstream, all three anglers in that direction had hooked fish, too.

Once Hilde and I were on the upper river on an August afternoon when much the same thing happened. Hilde was fishing Redman and I was up on the bank by the car watching when the rain began to fall that day. I'd lost sight of her fly behind a leafy maple branch, but I suddenly saw a steelhead—a really big steelhead—swimming fast and straight, from the middle of the river toward the roadside bank. When it made a quick turn and started back toward midstream, Hilde's reel began screaming. She lost that fish, but hooked another within a minute or two, and landed and released it, and then hooked a third steelhead just as quickly. By the time she'd released that one, the rain had stopped and the clouds were gone. We didn't raise another fish that day.

I've read that there is no logical reason to expect low barometric pressure to affect the behavior of fish. Logic or not, it definitely happens.

What are the best places to fish?

Anyone who fishes any river over a period of time will likely end up with favorite places. But this doesn't necessarily mean they are always the best places. In fact, having favorite places can sometimes result in hooking fewer fish, if you keep trying them even when they don't (or can't) produce. At Steamboat Inn one afternoon, a young man came in from one of the campgrounds with a very perplexed look on his face. He wanted to talk to Frank about his fishing. (Lots of people do.)

"I can't understand it," he said. "Last summer I hooked a fish at Williams Creek just about every time I went there, morning or night. This year I'm spending hours there every day, and I can't hook a thing."

"How long have you been here?" Frank asked him.

"Almost a week."

"You should've come in earlier. They won't be holding at Williams Creek this year. The water's too high."

It was as simple as that, and it reveals a very important fact about the North Umpqua: Things change from year to year, from week to week, from day to day.

Jack Hemingway has called the Camp Water "the best stretch of summer steelhead river in America." This may be true, but it's also true that the hot spots in the Camp Water change constantly. I remember a year when, because winter storms had scoured the gravel out of its lower end, the Hayden Run held more catchable fish than anywhere else. The following year, when the gravel had filled back in, hardly anyone hooked a steelhead there.

If a vote was taken on the best pool on the entire river, The Station would probably win, but there are years when even it is slow—sometimes because high water in Steamboat Creek makes it unnecessary for fish to hold there, other years for no readily apparent reason.

I can vividly remember different years when virtually every Camp Water spot—the Upper Boat, the Lower Boat, the Upper Kitchen, the Kitchen, the Fighting Hole, the Middle Mott, the Lower Mott, the Glory Hole—was the hot spot. The same is true downstream. The Ledges, the Log Pool, Split Rock, Burnham, Wright Creek, Fairview, these and others have their years—but certainly not every year.

It isn't merely a yearly thing either. Sometimes a place will hold fish consistently for weeks or days, and then, because of a drop in water level or temperature, everything suddenly stops. Just as often, it stops for a reason, or reasons, no one can identify. During a recent summer, lower Fairview held fish nearly every day through July and half of August, in a place where they could easily be spotted from the road. After mid-August no fish held there, and the few we hooked at Fairview came from behind a certain rock about thirty feet upstream.

Some spots—the Hayden Run and The Ledges come to mind—seem especially productive late in the evening, when it is dark enough for bats to be out: perfect choices for night people like Rob Carey. Others—Archie Creek and Fairview, for example—are almost always best at first light (perhaps because the first person through them is likely to either hook or spook most of the fish holding there).

So yes, there are indeed best places to fish, but no one can predict which ones they will be next year, next month, or even this afternoon.

How big do North Umpqua steelhead get?

The answer to even this question changes over the years. In the early 1970s, North Umpqua fish probably averaged six or eight pounds, with the largest fish arriving in May and June (the early run of natives that is now much depleted). Ten years later, the overall average was more like eight or nine pounds, with the increase due to hatcheries. I'm not sure it's accurate to say that these hatcheries have improved their practices, but they have changed them. As a result, planted steelhead are a lot bigger than they used to be and bigger on average than the native fish they share the river with. Before any steelhead smolts were released into the North Umpqua, a ten-pound fish was something of an event. Now a ten-pounder is fairly commonplace.

But there have always been a few big steelhead out there, just enough of them to allow a fisherman to keep the idea of a fifteen-pounder tucked into the back of his mind — and a real optimist will allow himself something even larger.

Frank Moore hooked an early-run fish in the Kitchen once, a heavy, obstinate fish that went straight to the bottom after the strike and held there immovably. When a minute or two had passed, he assumed it was a salmon, so he straightened the rod and reeled the line tight to break it off. Then it rolled, and it wasn't a salmon. The big June steelhead finally broke off, and Frank estimated its weight at close to thirty pounds. (He has a photo of the biggest North Umpqua fish he ever killed—a hook-jawed male—in his log house. He didn't weigh it , but it looks like a good twenty pounds or more to me.)

In late October 1992, Dan Callaghan was fishing all alone at the Lower Mott at nightfall when he landed and released a fish he is certain weighed twenty pounds. The following year a friend of mine, Don Zupan, landed a fish the same size at exactly the same place.

A Steamboat Inn guest named Chuck Tannlund hooked one of the big fish at The Ledges on an August morning. He fought it for more than half an hour, and jumped in and swam down the river after it before the leader finally broke at the fly. Chuck and friends who were with him guessed a weight near thirty pounds.

Nineteen eighty-seven produced the biggest run of summer fish since records have been kept—more than 20,000 passed over Winchester Dam—and the run included some big ones. On a mid-July morning, just as the river was dropping after an unseasonal rainstorm, I watched Hilde fish the Sawtooth. She hooked a fish that had been holding tight against the trailside ledge, and twenty minutes later, I helped her ease it into shallow water. It was a native male, the brightest and thickest fish I've ever seen anywhere that far from the ocean. I don't know how fast they can travel—no one really knows—but I can't believe that a steelhead that bright (a very faint trace of pink was barely visible along the lateral line) could have been out of salt water more than a week. (Frank Moore remembers checking some tagged fish around 1950; under normal water conditions, they took ten to fourteen days from Winchester Dam to Steamboat—a distance of about fifty river miles.) In any case, the bright male Hilde landed was just over a yard long and must have weighed between sixteen and seventeen pounds.

They get big enough.

October Caddis

5

Footnote on Flies

*He lit it and tossed the match into
the fast water below the logs. A tiny trout rose at the match,
as it swung around in the fast current.*

ERNEST HEMINGWAY
"Big Two-Hearted River"

THERE ARE A FEW OCCASIONS on our coastal rivers when we actually get to "match the hatch"—most often when the stone flies in June or the caddis flies in April or October are on the water and trout are rising to them. Much more often, though, we fish for steelhead with attractor patterns. When I started in the 1960s, fly selection was a relatively simple matter of pattern and size. If a big bright fly (say a Golden Demon) didn't raise fish, maybe a small dark one (perhaps a Black Prince) would. (On the North Umpqua, anything larger than 2 rates as big, and anything from 6 on down is small.) For many decades, the most popular fly on the river by far was a Skunk, usually size 4 or 6. (About two decades ago, Skunks began to appear with green butts.) Roderick Haig-Brown wrote that on the North Umpqua the Skunk, which has always been Frank Moore's favorite fly, "would outfish anything you cared to put against it." He also wrote, as have many others, that presentation of the fly is far more crucial than the pattern presented.

All of these conclusions seem perfectly sound to me, and if things remained today as they once were, there wouldn't be a lot left to say on the subject. But flies have changed over the past couple of decades, at least as much as rods and lines have.

I know a seventy-year-old who began fishing in his teens with a split-cane rod made by his father, a silk line that he braided himself, and traditional flies tied exclusively with materials that he gathered through his own hunting and scavenging. Today, of course, he uses a graphite rod that was quite possibly made by a robot, a line composed of who-knows-what, and flies that sometimes really do defy close description.

When I sold flies at the Steamboat Inn, we carried Skunks, Thors, Muddlers, Golden Demons, Black Princes, Bucktail Coachmen, Umpqua Specials, Cummings, and a few of the standard wet and dry patterns for trout. There were well-known local experts—call them artists—who tied these flies: Cal Bird, Stan Knouse, Joe Howell. These tiers worked with fur and feathers, tinsel and chenille. I went along with tradition and recommended size 4 Skunks to customers who weren't sure what they wanted. "They're a perfect compromise," I explained. "That's why they're so popular and why they usually work—not too big and not too small, or too bright or too dark either."

If you look through the fly selection at the Steamboat Inn today you will find grotesque creations with enough lead in them to fracture a skull; double-hooked, articulated maribou leeches five inches long; flies made of various synthetic materials that cause them to blink, glimmer, pulsate, shine, and maybe even wiggle and dance. I've fished with many of these modern patterns, and I've caught steelhead with them. They definitely have their times and places.

But somehow I never feel quite right about it when I use them, I suppose because I'm too old, or too old-fashioned, to forsake the traditional patterns. It's also true that I can't convince myself that these space-age flies are really all that much better than a Skunk, Thor, or Muddler.

I can trace my reluctance to place a lot of importance on fly pattern back to 1971, which was when I made my one-and-only contribution to fly tying by inventing the Right-Wing Special. Both the name of the fly and the pattern were offered to the well-to-do and mostly Republican Steamboat Inn guests in a spirit of good-natured fun.

The fly was tied to imitate a tiny American flag, with a red tail, a body made of bands of red, white, and blue chenille, a wing formed of layers of red, white, and blue bucktail, and a red head.

I gave out dozens of them over the summer and used them myself. I sincerely believe that, per hours fished, they caught as many steelhead as any other pattern. Stan Knouse finally tied a few dozen up and offered them for sale, and people actually bought them. I still keep a few in my fly box, and they still catch steelhead, but I don't know of anybody else who continues to use them. (Jeanne Moore keeps one as a souvenir.) Given the political climate these days, though, perhaps the time is right for the pattern to make a comeback.

But the real point is that if a Right-Wing Special can catch a steelhead, just about anything can.

The Racks Pool from downstream

Surveyor's Pool
from Mott Bridge

Autumn steelhead

Spot "X" during a snowstorm

Rip Rap Pool

Aerial view of Th
Upper, Middle
and Lower Mott Poo
in the Campwater abov
Steamboat In

The falls viewed across the
river from Steamboat Inn

6

Spice of the River

No pleasure endures unseasoned by variety.

PUBLILIUS SYRUS
Maxim 406

I'D SPENT A LONG, HOT AFTERNOON and evening in August fishing the upper river, and nothing had worked—not big flies or small ones, wets or dries, bright patterns or drab. Apparently it was just one of those frequent days when the steelhead won't move for anything. (Whenever that happens, I end up wondering how many fish I've covered in a morning or an evening; probably at least a dozen or fifteen; quite possibly twenty or more.)

The river at Fox Creek

On the way back downstream toward Island Campground, I pulled onto the shoulder of the road about a mile and a half below Apple Creek. There was just enough daylight left for me to observe a personal ritual, begun long ago; fishing at least one place each day that I've never tried before. It's a good way to avoid the questionable habit of going only to well-known pools, or the comfortable rut of returning again and again to the spots where you've caught fish. In the thirty miles of fly water, I'll certainly never run out of new opportunities. There must be literally thousands of pockets, boulders, ledges, riffles, and runs, many of them very hard to get to. While it's true that usually, after a hard or even dangerous climb down a steep bank, or a sweaty fight through thick brush, I find myself somewhere that is too shallow or too fast or too slow to hold steelhead, every once in a while—often enough to make it well worthwhile—I make a valuable discovery.

The random new place I'd picked today wasn't so bad: a short climb down a rocky bank to a fast, deep, fairly narrow run of water. It didn't really look promising at all, but at least there were no alder trees or streamside maples to get in the way of a backcast.

By the time I'd climbed down and found a fairly level rock at the river's edge to cast from, it was nearly dark. The well-known rule of thumb about steelhead water is that if it's too fast to wade comfortably, it's too fast to fish. The water I was looking at was so fast that a healthy young elephant might have had a hard time wading across it comfortably. Near the opposite bank, though—only twenty-five or thirty feet away—was a submerged car-sized boulder, its smoothly rounded top just inches beneath the surface.

I worked out line quickly and cast my big Muddler a few feet above the boulder. To my great surprise, a good fish turned behind it as it drifted by. All I could see in that light was the quick flash of a side; but it was a broad, bright side.

I cast again, and it rose again and this time struck at the Muddler. Two quick tugs and then it was gone.

After three more casts failed to bring another rise, I changed to a Thor and tried. But three more casts with it brought no response.

It was really dark now—I couldn't even see the boulder anymore—but I waited anyway, for at least five minutes.

With another yard of line stripped off, I cast the Thor a few extra feet above the cross-stream boulder to give it time to sink. This time the strike was one heavy pull, and the old Hardy Perfect reel sounded even louder than usual in the darkness.

The fish ran straight down the middle of the river for fifteen or twenty yards, stopped for a second or two, then ran another ten yards and stopped for good.

In that fast, heavy current, it was impossible to guess how big it might be, but I was sure all my knots were strong, and I reeled it steadily back upstream. Then, when I could see the butt of my leader, when I looked for the fish itself through the dark water, it ran again, back across the river to the boulder it had started from.

It is big, I told myself. Take it easy.

With a steady pressure, I drew the fish out from behind the boulder, then let it run with the current back downstream, like an instant replay: fifteen yards, a brief pause, then ten more.

The second time I reeled back up, it came all the way. What I finally saw surprised me as much as any fish I've ever caught anywhere: a brown trout, a thick-bodied, hook-jawed male at least two feet long. I've caught brown trout in a fair number of places, including native fish from a clear, cold stream in the mountains of Bavaria, but this was without question the loveliest one I've seen.

It wasn't really brown at all, but golden—as golden, I thought to myself, as a freshly boated dorado on the Sea of Cortez.

I knelt on the rock I'd cast from, the rod behind me now, one hand holding the leader, the other gripping the wrist of the tail. Even in the darkness, perhaps because of the darkness, the big trout shimmered with life, glowed with it. The crimson spots that marked the broad side were largest on the gill plate. The tail was somewhat smaller than a rainbow's, the dorsal fin much larger. The big mouth opened and closed, opened and closed.

Again glad to be using a barbless hook, I easily twisted the Thor from the hard roof of the mouth and lowered the brown trout down into the cool water—and took one more long look before I let go.

I'm sure I'm as glad as anybody that the North Umpqua has a run of summer steelhead, but if the river wasn't so famous for these fish—if it didn't have them—I think it would soon acquire a reputation for its other species of trout. The resident trout are there; it's just that, with steelhead available nearly all year long, hardly anyone has ever seriously fished for them.

I first became aware of the other trout in the river in a strange way. When my son Pete was nine years old, I began taking him fishing with me occasionally, but only when I felt the odds were very good that I could hook a steelhead. Then, when I did hook one, I would let him try to land it. Youngsters become bored easily, and my reasoning was that, familiar with the excitement of playing a big fish, he might be capable of adequate patience when he tried to hook one himself.

That strategy worked out as planned, but not until we'd had a few minor misadventures.

Late one July afternoon I had Pete under the Mott Bridge, on the trailside ledge, where, with sun on the smooth water, I'd spotted two steelhead holding just downstream earlier that day. After I'd covered the lie with a Skunk, and covered it again, giving gentle motion to the fly, I reeled in and handed the rod to Pete, standing downstream to my left.

"Hold onto it a minute," I said, "while I find another fly to try."

I looked through two boxes wondering what to choose and finally decided on a Spruce, a pattern I'd always had a lot of luck with on the Klamath in the fall. The long, slender feather wings might move well in the gentle current here.

"What's that big bird?" Pete asked me.

I looked up. "A heron," I said. "A blue heron."

His wide eyes watched it flap upstream on slow, measured wing beats.

Then—when I reached for my rod—I saw that his hands were empty.

"Where's my rod?"

"I don't know." His voice was bewildered, his face the picture of innocence.

Watching the heron, he had simply forgotten the rod and dropped it into the river. I stared down into the water, but even with Polaroids, it was hopeless. That is a deep run, and the only way to see the bottom clearly is from up on the bridge under the midday sun.

I give myself some credit. I didn't blow up—at least not outwardly. But in those days I owned only one moderately decent rod and one dependable reel, so their loss was significant.

"We'll look from up above," I said. We climbed up the steep bank and walked out onto the bridge, but I couldn't see a thing through the dark, deep water.

"We'll head back to the inn," I said. "I'll get my diving mask."

"I'm sorry," Pete said.

"So am I," I answered, and we headed back.

The whole thing turned out to have not just one happy ending, but two.

When I swam down the hundred yards or so of water between the bridge and the Sawtooth Pool with my diving mask, I didn't find my rod and reel or spot any steelhead, but I did go over hundreds of trout, including some big ones. I'd hooked trout now and then while steelhead fishing, of course—everyone has—but I'd never imagined so many down there. I thought it was a valuable discovery, and I was so impressed that, despite the cold water, I walked back up the ledge to the bridge and swam down to see them again.

Then, the next morning, Fred Boyle, a friend from Bend who often fishes with a sinking line, snagged my rod across the river in the Station Pool, landed it, and returned it to me, none the worse for its overnight soaking.

That evening Pete and I used it to cast small wet caddis imitations to the trout I'd seen, and we each caught our share of them.

I've been fishing the river fairly seriously and fairly often for trout ever since.

The brown hooked by accident below Apple Creek is still the biggest resident trout I've ever caught on the North Umpqua, but not by much. There have been several browns of sixteen and eighteen inches, many smaller than that, two or three larger ones. Many of them come from a deep, slow run of water a little ways above Dry Creek, but just last summer (1994) I was fooled again at the Log Pool, about two miles below Steamboat Creek. I hooked a good fish at first light in the morning, just off the rock point where steelhead usually hold, and I didn't know it was a big brown instead of a small steelhead until I had it close enough to see.

All North Umpqua brown trout are remarkably healthy and beautiful fish. (Dan Callaghan, who's caught many more of them than I have, in many more places, also says that North Umpqua browns are the prettiest he's ever seen.) The species was originally introduced to the river in the 1930s or 1940s—apparently no one knows exactly why or when—but none have been planted since then, so for all practical purposes they have become native fish; and it's obvious that their environment suits them very well.

And these brown trout make the North Umpqua a truly unique river, because both rainbows and cutthroats (including sea-run cutthroats as well as steelhead) are native to the watershed. Few rivers anywhere give a fisherman the chance of hooking all three species of true trout on earth. (The Fish and Wildlife Department also plants eight- to ten-inch rainbows early each summer, off the Wright Creek and Apple Creek bridges. If these have any use, it is to teach youngsters to fly fish or to provide a quick and easy campground meal.)

Probably the best time to set out to catch trout is in the spring and early summer, which is just as well, because that is the slowest time for steelhead, anyway. But I carry a box of trout flies all the time now, because opportunities can come unexpectedly. A few years ago, when Hilde and I were fishing together on a slow, sunny October afternoon, a caddis hatch began. Before long there were clouds of the little flies around us. Trout soon began to feed everywhere, and I had some elk-hair caddis imitations that saved our day.

The best place to catch trout is on the upper river, above Steamboat Creek, and this is especially true of browns. In my experience, rainbows and cutthroats are scattered everywhere. Depending on water conditions, any of the standard trout techniques will work: dries, wets, nymphs, streamers.

It's also possible to compromise, which is what I often do in June by using a dark, somewhat oversized trout fly—a size 6 Woolly Worm, perhaps—that is perfectly adequate for steelhead. A few Junes ago, on just that fly, I hooked some native rainbows, an eighteen-inch cutthroat, a twenty-pound chinook and a six-pound steelhead between six and eight in the evening. The cutthroat came from the Station Pool and was probably one that had drifted down out of Steamboat Creek in high water. The salmon came from Fairview, and that fish, a silvery-bronze female, is the real reason I remember the evening so well. She had no tail—probably thanks to a sea lion or seal near the mouth of the river—and the stump had healed and grown over smoothly. She fought remarkably well anyway, but the real wonder of it is that a fish that size without a tail could make it up all those miles of roaring river in apparent good health. (For many years the world record sport-caught chinook, an eighty-nine pounder, came from the Umpqua, until it was finally displaced by an Alaska fish. Hooking a big chinook on a floating line in the fly water certainly isn't common, but it's happened to nearly every experienced North Umpqua fisherman more than once.)

Learning to see the North Umpqua as a trout river as well as a steelhead river has increased both my enjoyment and appreciation. In future years, I plan to test its varied possibilities more thoroughly than I have so far.

Burnt Creek Pool

7

The Gentleman at Fairview

The purest joy of all is the joy of nature.

LEO TOLSTOY
in a letter to his wife

WE ALL KNOW that humans mature as they grow older, and not just physically; we also know that different individuals reach remarkably different levels of maturity. These same observations can be applied in obvious ways to fishermen: Serious anglers are apt to go through a number of identifiable stages in their development, and this is particularly true of fly fishermen, simply because, as a group, they are the most dedicated and passionate anglers of all.

Most often, in the beginning, we want to catch a lot of fish; then big fish; then difficult fish, or rare fish, or different kinds of fish than we have caught before, or more of the same kinds of fish we have caught before but in different places. Even today, despite all the compelling arguments against it, many beginning fishermen are determined to kill what they catch and show it to someone to prove that they have been somewhere and done something. But if they stay with it for long, and particularly if they fish with flies, they begin to release some fish, or most fish, or all but trophy fish, or all but hatchery fish, or everything.

If we can call all of this a process of maturity, then the most mature angler I've ever met was an elderly gentleman I ran into at Fairview eighteen or twenty years ago. Watching from the bank, I saw him raise and miss two nice fish in the upper end of the pool. Then, when I talked to him after he had finished, he explained that missing fish was no disappointment. He had clipped all the points off his flies and was happy to fish only for strikes.

"Why did you decide to do that?" I asked him. "Because you don't want to hurt the fish?"

"No, not that," he answered. "I've read a lot of Thoreau."

He looked at me and I nodded at him, to indicate that I'd read Thoreau too, and then he went on.

"I think it was in *Walden* where he wrote that a lot of men fish all their lives without ever realizing that fish isn't really what they're after. Well, a while back, I figured out that he was right, at least in my case. The fish are just a reasonable excuse to be out here. If I worry about them too much, I miss a lot of everything else—of what I'm really here for." The old man smiled happily. "Does that make any sense?"

"Sure," I said. "I remember that passage. I know what you mean."

But I was fairly young, then, and I didn't really quite believe in what he was trying to tell me. In fact, as soon as he'd left, I climbed down the bank to fish for the two steelhead he'd raised and was very happy to hook and land one of them.

Now, years later and no longer young, I still enjoy hooking and landing fish; but I also think I finally know what the old man meant, and I appreciate it—and (I hope I can explain this) the appreciation actually seems to be retroactive.

Fifteen years ago—even ten—if asked about my most vivid memories of the North Umpqua, I would immediately have thought of the biggest or wildest fish I'd ever hooked, or of those very rare days (two or maybe three in a decade) when aggressive steelhead could be found in virtually every riffle and pool.

I still remember certain fish and certain days, and it makes me happy to know I'll always have those memories; but when I think back now over the years many other things are apt to come to mind.

On the trail side of the upper river, at a fairly remote place I know, a sleek river otter and the two small pups she was herding ahead of her slid over the lip of a waterfall with power and grace more effortless than any I've ever seen on a basketball court or athletic field.

As I sat on a warm streamside rock near Discovery, waiting for the sun to slide a little farther down in the sky, a fifty-pound beaver swam by me not five feet away, heading upstream toward the Log Pool. Without thinking about it, I said, "Hello." He turned his head to stare at me, an inquisitive look in his bright brown eyes, dense dark fur beaded with water. He stared at me for at least a minute, swimming just hard enough in the current to hold his own. "You might as well go on," I finally told him, and he did, swimming upstream as unconcerned as he had been before we spoke.

About halfway up the trail from Wright Creek to Rattlesnake, on a dark early morning, I thought I saw another fisherman, a surprisingly short, fat man, walking toward me down the trail. I had my mouth open to say hello when I suddenly realized that it wasn't a fisherman, it was a bear. Just as I stopped walking, he did. Then he stood on his hind legs, wheeled around smoothly, dropped down to all fours, and lumbered back upstream. I went back toward Wright Creek, as wide awake as I've ever been at that hour.

(Frank Moore's nephew had a somewhat more exciting encounter at the Log Pool not long ago. He was wading deep, as you need to do there, when he heard something splashing in the shallow water behind him. When he turned, he saw a frolicking cougar, and when he yelled—a combination of surprise and fright—the big, wet cat trotted up the steep trail to the road and disappeared.)

There are deer and elk along the river, osprey and water ouzels, quail and grouse. In fall, on the best days after the maples have turned, when the big bronze chinook are spawning on the shallow gravel bars, simply watching the river can give more pleasure than fishing it.

A long time ago, there was a rare winter day with two or three inches of fresh powder snow along the riverbanks, and with the cold blue-green water free of algae, and thus clearer and more lovely than in summer. As I waded into a pool above Copeland Creek a flock of whistling swans flew overhead in an elongated V, their stretched necks as long as their bodies, their wing spans six or seven feet, black bills and white undersides in sharp detail against a cold gray sky, so close that I heard the rushing hiss of their slow, powerful wing beats as they passed. I don't remember if I caught a fish, but that day and those swans will always be with me.

So I've come to see the river not merely—or even mostly—as a place to catch fish, but as a great work of art, a living painting composed by God or Nature—choose your term. It may be that from a fishing point of view, the steelhead remains the central subject of this picture. But it is a complex painting, with much more than a single subject to it; all the other fish, the birds and animals, the big trees, the rich sounds and living colors—these are the essential background, the solid and perfect frame that give true meaning and completeness.

Surveyor's Pool with snow

8

———

Green Water,
White Snow

There is no season such delight can bring,
As summer, autumn, winter, and the spring.

WILLIAM BROWNE
"Variety"

FOR MANY NORTH UMPQUA FISHERMEN, and this is particularly true of recent years, the most attractive time of the year is fall. To show how things have changed regarding popular seasons over the past decade or so, I can briefly recount another of my old traditions; going to the river on Labor Day evening. It wasn't much more than ten years ago that Hilde and I arrived about two hours before dark on that day to discover that, as we'd hoped, the traditional long-weekend crowds had disappeared entirely.

So we had our pick of places to fish and chose Archie Creek, where I sat on the high rock and watched Hilde hook and land two fine steelhead. Satisfied with her success, she slept late on Tuesday morning, and I got up early and went straight back to Archie, without seeing another fisherman on the two-mile upriver drive. I had a strong feeling there would be more steelhead in the pool, so I fished it even more slowly and carefully than usual—and the feeling proved to be right. I hooked three steelhead and landed two of them. When I drove back downstream to an unnamed place not far below Fairview, there were still no other fishermen out. I landed two more steelhead there and then quit, more than satisfied. I was back in the cabin making coffee before Hilde woke up. We stayed three days on that trip and had very good fishing the whole time on a nearly deserted river.

The opening day of deer season in October used to be another good time to fish, but there's nothing special about it anymore. Nowadays, whether the fishing is good, bad, or mediocre, the river is almost sure to be as crowded all through September and October as it was in July and August—ironically, crowded mostly with people who have come to beat the crowds. November storms sweeping in from the coast are likely to put the river out of shape for days at a time, but if Indian-summer weather comes instead, the fishermen come with it and stay at least until Thanksgiving.

That leaves winter fishing, which, by standard definition, begins in December. It is the only time left when the North Umpqua can truly be called uncrowded. Considering that the winter season is five months long—healthy fish can often be caught well into April—it's certainly worth trying if you don't care for crowds and are willing to suffer some discomfort.

But before the discomfort, here are some things that are generally known—or at least believed—about winter fishing in the North Umpqua.

Winter steelhead are somewhat larger—or at least they average larger—than summer fish. Despite this, they are often unspectacular fighters, and the reason has a lot to do with water temperatures.

Years ago it was widely believed that a water temperature below thirty-eight degrees made fishing virtually pointless. Now, probably due in large part to modern fast-sinking lines, it is at least possible to hook fish no matter how cold the water is. I know two fishermen who have caught steelhead when the river measured thirty-one degrees, which means they were fishing in what could be called liquid ice. But the fight of such a fish, or of any steelhead caught in water under forty degrees, will almost surely be a disappointment. Three or four degrees above forty, though, and the same logy fish might jump and run wildly when hooked.

As a general rule, cold water means fast-sinking lines and weighted flies, because a steelhead with a barely functioning metabolism won't move very far for anything. And yet, for reasons that I don't think have ever been convincingly explained by anybody, air temperature often appears to be at least as important as water temperature. Given a choice between a day with fairly warm water but fairly cold air, or one with fairly cold water but fairly warm air, I would choose the latter every time. I think this is why February and March are the most popular months with most experienced winter fishermen. The days are growing longer, then, with more sun on the water. We always have periods of warm weather, often a so-called false spring. These conditions make steelhead surprisingly responsive. I've raised many fish from deep winter pools to a barely sunken fly fished on a floating line when the air was warm.

An ideal winter fishing day, then, would be one with balmy air and low, clear, fairly warm water. Unfortunately, such days are rare.

Usually by December there is considerable snow in the Cascade Mountains—often four or five feet, sometimes a good deal more—at elevations above six thousand feet. (At winter's end, the runoff from this snowpack will become the river in which we catch our summer steelhead.)

Northwest winter weather is constantly changing, and whenever the air warms substantially, some snow melts. If rain accompanies warm air, which is a typical pattern, rain and melted snow combine, and rivers are soon high and muddy with the warmed water through which winter steelhead move upstream.

At least once or twice each year flooding will occur. It is a good and healthy thing because it scours out the riverbed, removing accumulated debris and cleaning and redistributing gravel—and sometimes uprooting huge trees and rolling massive boulders along the riverbed as if they were gigantic bowling balls. It is always surprising how a river you think you know well becomes almost unrecognizable in winter flood. A favorite place that was lovely and inviting not long ago, under summer sun, can be downright frightening with the volume of water tripled or quadrupled.

A return of cold air after a storm will stop the snowmelt and lower the river, and this dropping water cools off quickly. Steelhead that have been moving upstream in high water will begin to settle into pockets and pools. The inevitable result of these natural conditions is that a winter fisherman often has to choose between a relatively warm day with high and discolored water, or a cold day with low, cold, clear water.

The brief transitional periods often offer the best chance of finding something close to the ideal: the two or three days after a storm has ended, when the water drops and begins to clear, and the fish stop moving while the air remains at least mild.

I remember just such a February day when Hilde and I fished together. We were staying at the Steamboat Inn as guests of the Moores, who had driven up to Diamond Lake to cross-country ski with a friend. The river was beginning to drop nicely after a three-day storm, but Steamboat Creek was still running muddy, so we decided to fish the cleaner water upstream. This is typical of the North Umpqua in winter: The tributary creeks that have been logged heavily silt the river, so the farther upstream you go, the better the water looks. When the Camp Water is unfishable, conditions might be fine five miles up.

We drove up the lonely road under a gray sky, the country damp and cold looking, patches of snow along the rocky banks, smokelike clouds of shifting white mist in the steep canyons against the green trees, and the high mountains covered with snow. I parked above Apple Creek. From the bank I could barely see two steelhead through the green water, both eight- or nine-pounders, holding side by side over gravel in a run above the bridge. I helped Hilde down the rocky ledge and out onto the point we fish from. Casting a slow-sinking line, she covered the pair of fish with a big bright Umpqua Special. Then I tried it with a fast-sinking shooting head and a Muddler, but neither fish moved. By the time we climbed back to the car, my hands and feet were numb, despite insulated socks and gloves. When Hilde told me she wasn't cold I made a joke about women having more body fat than men—I should add here that she was, and is, in excellent shape—but she didn't think it was very funny. We drove upstream, talking about the river.

We decided to try Charcoal Point. This far up the water was noticeably clearer than it had been at Apple Creek. Hilde fished the middle of the pool, concentrating on the big rock about twenty feet off the bank, and I covered as much of the water above that as I could reach.

"Cold yet?" I asked as we climbed back up to the car.

"A little."

"I don't mind it with my feet so much, but I can't cast when my hands get numb. I can hardly hold onto the rod. It's nice out, though. Nobody else around."

We went all the way up to Copeland Creek so Hilde could fish the run below the creek mouth, often one of the best winter steelhead spots on the river. A light, steady snow had begun to fall, big, wet flakes slowly drifting straight down in the windless canyon. Once Hilde was on a comfortable rock and had begun to cast, I watched the flakes as they hit the dark water and dissolved.

"Mike!"

She had hooked a steelhead on her third or fourth cast. (Now, after a quarter century of fishing and hundreds of steelhead, Hilde's excitement at hooking a fish has never diminished—and I love her for her enthusiasm.)

"I'll never land it!" she said (that old combination of hope and desperation that, no matter how long we have fished, all of us sometimes feel).

"Sure, you will," I answered.

"It's big!"

"Don't worry, this is a big pool. It isn't going anywhere."

"It struck hard, as soon as the fly hit the water!"

"Take it easy," I said. "You'll land it."

And several minutes later, she did.

It was big enough, over ten pounds, and lovely, too—a native fish, a well-colored male. As I held it gently to admire it after the hook had been twisted out, the falling snowflakes dusted his strong, shimmering body.

As soon as I released my grip on the wrist of his tail, he was gone, down and then out, toward the middle of the river. Just then a car sped by on the road behind us, heading upstream, probably toward Diamond Lake. We noticed it only because it was the first one we had seen or heard that day.

We drove back downstream to Frankie's Favorite, named after Frank Moore's son, who was the first, or one of the first, to fish it regularly after the river above Mott Bridge was opened to fall and winter angling in 1971. It is a long riffle reached by a steep, narrow trail through old-growth forest that includes some of the biggest sugar pines I've ever seen. It is far enough off the road so that, if you try, it's easy to imagine you have gone back into the true wilderness that the Upper North Umpqua country was, not so very long ago.

Hilde had her fish, so she stayed on the bank and watched me wade out, trying to get just far enough to ignore the streamside alders. (I don't care to roll cast a sinking line unless I have to.) The snow had stopped, and the water was much clearer now than when we had begun to fish—I could easily see my boots when I was waist-deep — but seemed colder, too. My feet were really numb, and I leaned upstream into the current as I inched my way out over the gravel. (I realized I was wading over the next generation of chinook salmon, the fertilized eggs buried safely ten or twelve inches underneath the gravel.)

It took me a good quarter hour to methodically fish the lower half of the deep riffle: a cast and a quick mend, then the long cross-stream swing, another step downstream, and cast again.

I finally found my fish at the very bottom, almost straight below me.

It wasn't nearly as big as Hilde's, or quite as wild, but that might have been just as well because my hands were so cold and useless when I hooked it, they could barely work the reel. But I managed to stumble back in underneath the bare, wet alder branches, and to land the fish and release it in good shape.

What I remember most vividly about the day came afterward. We drove straight back to the inn, where I took a quick hot shower and changed into warm clothes. The Moores weren't back yet; so while Hilde showered, I went up to the dining room and built up the fire with some well-seasoned chunks of red fir and a log of madrone.

Then I poured two inches of good bourbon into a clear glass and sat there close to the big stone fireplace in the spreading warmth. I was waiting for my wife, and we had both caught steelhead. Bourbon never tasted better. I never enjoyed a fire more. Winter fishing did it.

Lower end of Camp Water from Point at Steamboat Inn

9

Divided by Three

*One cannot know intimately all the ways and movements
of a river without growing into love of it.*

RODERICK HAIG-BROWN
A River Never Sleeps

WHEN WE SPEAK of the North Umpqua fly water—and even when we think
about it—most of us divide it into three neat sections: the Camp Water, the
river below the Camp Water, and the river above it.

I

The Camp Water—the series of pools, runs, and riffles between Mott Bridge and Steamboat Inn—may indeed be the finest stretch of summer steelhead water in America; but it has also become, through much of the year, one of the most heavily fished stretches of summer steelhead water in America, and that can definitely be a problem.

Mornings in particular seem to bring out the most determined and competitive fishermen. In mid-July it is possible to see well enough to fish effectively at a little before 5:00 a.m. I can remember many mornings when, driving by the Lower Boat Pool on the highway and looking across toward the heart of the Camp Water, I saw two or three glowing cigarettes and three or four flashlights distributed among the various pools. Jack Hemingway is said to have outmaneuvered these early risers by spending nights sleeping (or trying to sleep) with his fly rod on the rocks near the head of the Station Pool, to be sure he got to fish it first in the morning. (The Station is the river's most popular spot of them all, and I've come to believe that within another two or three decades it will have been fished so often by so many that smooth grooves will appear in the rock ledges there, like those formed over ages in the stone staircases of medieval cathedrals.)

I don't know if anybody goes to Hemingway's lengths anymore, but I do know that in any good year at the height of the summer season you can cross the Mott Bridge and pull into the fishermen's parking lot at 4:30 and find six or eight vehicles already there. And if you happen to catch someone putting a rod up or lacing a boot at that hour, he will likely start down the trail at a fast walk or a clumsy trot before you switch your lights off, to be sure of reaching the river ahead of you. On such days, you can be certain there are already fishermen impatiently waiting in the dark at the Station, the Lower Boat, the Upper Kitchen, the Kitchen and the Middle Mott, and quite likely at some of the other pools besides.

There was a time when I would gladly try to get to the Camp Water first on a summer morning. If that failed—even if the parking lot was nearly full—I was willing to hurry down the trail behind all the others and fish wherever I could find a spot, or wait out whomever had arrived ahead of me at a place I was certain held steelhead. Nowadays I seldom even try to fish the Camp Water early. If I do try and find more than one or two people already there, I turn around and head downstream if it's July or upstream if it's August.

A Californian named Frank Morrel—not an early-morning person—solved the crowd problem as reasonably as anyone I've heard about. When he stayed at the inn, he slept until about 8:00 a.m., ate a leisurely and ample breakfast, and then drove to the Camp Water, fairly sure by that time that the early wave of anglers had subsided. Starting at the Sawtooth, he worked his way all the way down through the Mott, and he hooked plenty of fish that way—probably at least as many as any of the predawn people.

Fishing memories are important—more important all the time, I think, as we age. Now that I've fished the Camp Water hundreds or maybe thousands of times, the recollections evoked there give me even more pleasure than any fish I happen to hook; and something well worth remembering has happened to me, or to someone I was with, at every pool.

Walking down the narrow trail from the parking lot, the Sawtooth is the first place you come to, and that was where I watched Hilde hook, play, and land her more-than-a-yard-long steelhead in 1987.

Just below the Sawtooth break is the Hayden Run, named after the colonel, who hooked and lost a huge fish there in the late 1950s. Most people new to the river walk by without ever guessing steelhead might hold there, but in fairly low water they do, usually behind a few scattered rocks that give just enough protection from the swift current. Twenty-some years ago, well after dark, after everybody else had quit for the evening, I caught three big fish—all of them wild natives—from behind the rocks at the upper end of the run on three successive short casts.

Not all my Camp Water memories have to do with fish. Along the trail near the Hayden Run, in the late 1960s, the Forest Service conducted a well-named but ill-fated experiment in human comfort. They installed an outhouse called a "Destroylet." It appeared to be like any other outhouse until, after its use, the lid was closed. Then a roaring flame ignited, its purpose to incinerate whatever had been left there. The Destroylet

Upstream from The Racks Pool

View downstream from Mott Bridge;
Sawtooth Pool, Sweetheart Pool,
and Station Pool

Downstream from
Huckleberry Pool

Charcoal Point, angler
Hilde Baughman

Boundary Pool

Lower end of Boundary Pool

disappeared after a few months, and ever since I've wondered if possibly, somehow, the triggering device malfunctioned for some unfortunate angler and the flame ignited ahead of schedule. It's not a pleasant thought, and in any case it's probably best that the Destroylet is a small part of Camp Water history now, because if such an accident happened today, it would surely result in one of the most massive personal-injury lawsuits ever filed.

Just across the river from the former site of the Destroylet is the seldom-fished Sweetheart Hole, where Hilde landed the biggest sea-run cutthroat trout I've ever seen.

About fifteen yards below the Sweetheart is the famous Station. Of all the memories I have of the pool, the most vivid is of an evening I got Pete over there when he was eleven or twelve. Minutes after we arrived, the sun went down, and steelhead immediately began rolling up and down the length of the pool. He hooked three or four in as many casts and quickly lost them all when they ran down over the break into the long rapids. We had plenty of flies along, though, and I think he might have hooked three or four more if a tourist watching from his motor home parked on the shoulder of the highway hadn't clambered down the bank and out onto the roadside ledge, right on top of the fish. (To make matters worse, he was wearing a white shirt and an even whiter cowboy hat.) Using a spinning rod and plastic bubble, he splatted a fly down about two yards from his feet and, to our surprise and his, too, hooked a steelhead. It might have been the first of his life, because it excited him so much that he fell headfirst into the pool with an enormous splash. That ended our evening at the Station.

I watched Colonel Hayden land what I think was the last North Umpqua steelhead of his life at the Upper Boat, and I'm glad it was a good one. (He caught it late in the morning, with bright sun on the water, after three or four fishermen had already been through the water.) And of course I'll always remember my first North Umpqua fish from the Lower Boat, and Hilde's from the Kitchen.

Another memorable first-hooked-fish came from the Middle Mott, the same year the colonel hooked his last one. I was out in the early evening with a Steamboat Inn guest who had never fished for steelhead before, but who said he'd had a lot of experience with other trout. We had walked down the trail and were wading out across the shallow ledge to the Middle Mott before I noticed his automatic fly reel.

"I'm not so sure about that reel if you hook a big fish out here," I told him.

"Don't worry," he answered confidently. "I've caught all kinds of big trout in Colorado with it."

I didn't really know much about automatic reels—only that they were designed to retrieve line at the press of a lever—so I kept quiet after that despite my misgivings.

And that reel might have been fine on an average fish; but the one he hooked just a few minutes after he began to cast hit with one of those really powerful, wrenching strikes. Then it began its run downstream. Then, an instant before the line went slack, the automatic reel literally exploded. I remember thinking at the time that it was much like a scene in a cartoon: There was a kind of grinding, popping noise, and then reel parts flew in all directions—springs, screws, many small pieces of unidentifiable metal.

The look on his pale face, mouth half open and eyes glazed under a wide-brimmed hat, was memorable too: made up, I thought, of equal parts of amazement, excitement, and embarrassment.

"I guess your leader was a little heavy," I said finally.

Generations of anglers, thousands of steelhead, high adventures and comic mishaps: I suppose the Camp Water is a microcosm of the history of the river, and of steelhead fishing everywhere.

II

Just as nearly everyone starts his North Umpqua fishing at the Camp Water, nearly everyone who gets beyond this stage begins to learn the pools below the Camp Water next. The easiest way to discover the location of many of these spots is to remember where cars are parked or to spot visible fishermen as you drive (do it carefully) along the road. (It's also worth knowing that some very fine pools—the Pulpit, just above Archie Creek, and Cougar Creek, not far below Coleman—can't be seen from the road and have no parking pullouts near them, so seldom get the fishing pressure they deserve.)

Most of these productive places have been fished hard for decades and have old, well-known names: The Ledges, the Tree Pool, Leaning Tree (though the actual leaning tree washed out in high water years ago), Williams Creek, the Log Pool, Discovery, Split Rock, Burnham, Archie Creek, Lower Archie, Coleman, Cougar Creek, Rattlesnake, MacDonald, Wright Creek, Fairview, and so on, all the way down to the Famous Hole, just above the Rock Creek fly-water boundary.

There are two traditional ways to fish these downstream spots: by hiking along the narrow trail through ferns and huge old-growth trees along the south bank, or by driving the north-bank highway. During the summer months, vehicles race up and down the road between the pools every morning and evening, fly rods in their holders slanting back over the roofs or poking out the windows. There are surely exceptions, but I think these drivers are usually the competitive types who measure their success by numbers of hooked fish; while those who are content to relax and enjoy the river, and who count a hooked fish a pleasant bonus, are more apt to be found across the river on the relatively quiet and peaceful trail.

In recent years, to the dismay of many, a third alternative has emerged: fishing from a floating device is prohibited, but more and more anglers with float tubes or small rubber rafts are driving the road and crossing at well-chosen spots—just below Split Rock, for example—to fish the south bank. The dismay results when you walk two or three miles to reach the place you've been looking forward to fishing and then discover that someone who just paddled across in a raft is already there.

Another change: It used to be that when virtually every well-known spot between Steamboat Creek and Fall Creek had at least one fisherman in it, there would still be plenty of room, even some solitude, in various areas all the way down to Rock Creek. But the growing popularity of fly fishing has resulted in more local people from the Roseburg area fishing the lower reaches of the fly water now.

Still, a lot of river is available out there. Even on the most crowded weekends in July and August, there are good places if you look for them. The standard old advice is to fish the slicks above the rapids where the river deepens and the current spreads and slows; and the Log Pool, both Archie Creek and Lower Archie, Lower Burnham, Coleman, Rattlesnake, and Wright Creek are classic examples of this definition and proof that the old advice is good. It isn't the only good advice, though. There remain hundreds of unnamed pockets, runs, and riffles that hold steelhead, and it's possible to have a very enjoyable and successful day fishing places that simply look as though they could hold fish. Often they do. I'm convinced that the naming of pools inhibits many beginners, conditioning them to believe that they probably can't catch anything in a place that hasn't yet been dignified with a label. It's not only possible to hook steelhead in unnamed and unknown places; but because we have figured things out for ourselves, these are usually the most satisfying fish of all.

III

I often find myself reluctant to say or write much about the river above Steamboat Creek—fully one-third of the designated fly water—because I love it so much.

So, begin with the necessary warning: It can be a difficult—even dangerous—area to fish. Yes, there are some places where you can park, climb out of a car and stroll down a short, well-worn trail to an easy rock to fish from; but there are many more places without trails that demand a long, hard climb down to the river, and then some challenging wading before you can make your first cast. It really is best to go here with a friend, because accidents can happen—have happened—on the steep, rocky banks and slippery ledges.

The relative difficulty is the most obvious reason why the upper river is underfished. Another reason is the commonly held belief—not true—that nearly all steelhead that make it as far as the Camp Water turn up Steamboat Creek to spawn. No one can know the percentages for certain, but it's likely that at least thirty percent of the fish that cross Winchester Dam reach the upper river.

An obvious indication of the lack of fishing pressure is the fact that relatively few upriver spots have popular names. (This is due partly to the fact that the river above Mott Bridge has been open to late summer and fall and winter fishing for only twenty-five years.) Upper and Lower Redman and the Christmas Tree Pool below Apple Creek are widely known and often fished. The beaver Pool and Panther Leap above Apple Creek are known to old-timers and fished by them. Once we get above Dry Creek— nine miles upstream from Steamboat—most of the pool names (some whimsical, some descriptive) are those we have made up ourselves: Swiss Cheese (named after the slippery holes in the ledge you must wade across to fish it); Landslide (where I once slid forty or fifty yards down a steep slope, breaking a rod, ripping out brush and small trees with both hands, dirt and rocks sliding and bouncing down behind me); the Engagement Pool (where Ron Hansen asked our daughter Ingrid to be his wife).

Learning the upper river has been a lot like learning a new river: One important part of the process is disproving widely held beliefs. (It was once accepted as absolute fact that steelhead wouldn't take flies; that they wouldn't take dry flies; that they couldn't be caught in cold water; and so on.)

It is still believed by nearly everyone who does fish the upper North Umpqua that steelhead don't arrive there in significant numbers until

August. I believed this, too (though I'm really not sure why), until just a few years ago.

It was the second week in July, and because of my son Pete's work schedule we were fishing together on a weekend. On Friday evening we were surprised to find the pressure moderate enough to allow us to hook a fish apiece at the Camp Water (Pete's at the Station and mine at the Hayden Run), and then to hook two more downstream (at Split Rock and Fairview).

But Saturday morning was impossible. We were up early, as usual, and Pete fished Archie Creek while I went through Lower Archie, but neither of us raised a fish. From there we drove downstream all the way to Fox Creek and then back up to Steamboat. The river was as mobbed as I've ever seen it: vehicles parked at every pullout, dozens more speeding in both directions along the road looking for places to fish.

"To hell with this," I finally told Pete. "Let's try it upstream."

"Will there be steelhead up there yet?"

"No. But I'd rather not catch a fish by myself than deal with this."

"The trail looked pretty crowded, too."

"I noticed."

"We can come back here later," he said, "when everybody's quit for the morning. And we might pick up some nice trout up above."

By the time we had driven a mile past Steamboat it was as if we really were on a different river—or had crossed a border into another country—with no sign of a fisherman anywhere.

I dropped Pete off at Charcoal Point and started myself above Dry Creek at Swiss Cheese, but farther down the long run than usual, because I wasn't really expecting anything to happen. My first cast off the shallow ledge was so short that I didn't even have my entire leader out of the guides, and as the Skunk began its short swing, a six-inch smolt came up and pecked at it twice. Just as the smolt disappeared, my lazy attention was diverted momentarily by a low-flying merganser; but, from the corner of my eye, I saw the big, swirling boil on the calm water. Before I fully realized what had happened, my leader was out of the guides, along with ninety feet of fly line and some backing.

We found wild fish everywhere we stopped on the upper river that morning, and for the rest of the weekend, too. Their aggressiveness was proof to me that they had just arrived. Best of all, we had them to ourselves.

So when all the technical advice has been cataloged and analyzed, and the theory and speculation argued exhaustively, there remains only one certain rule to assure good fishing: Be at the right place at the right time.

Through pure luck—the water was neither high nor low, and the weather was normal—the right time came two or three weeks early that year. No doubt it's often happened before, and I'm sure it will happen again. Next time I won't be as surprised, but I'll be just as happy about it.

The upper river is the wildest and loveliest part of the North Umpqua, and there are two new developments—one good and one bad from a fisherman's viewpoint—that anybody wanting to fish there should know about.

Rafters and kayakers (the rubber hatch, some call it) are more numerous all the time during the warm months. No doubt they, too, come for the beauty, and because this section of river is steeper, with more rapids, and longer and faster ones, than can be found downstream. Some of these people are considerate to fishermen, while some of them aren't—most often, I suspect, because they know little or nothing about fishing. They aren't often out in the cool early mornings; but on a normal evening, at least a dozen kayaks and a raft or two will bounce and glide over the water you're fishing, or would like to fish.

(There are guidelines, posted by the Forest Service at streamside takeout points, such as the gravel pit just below Island Campground. The water from the gravel pit to Bogus Creek is supposed to be closed to rafters from July 15 to October 31, and the water from Soda Springs to the gravel pit and from Bogus Creek down is supposed to be closed every day from 6:00 p.m. until 10:00 a.m. Yet there are some who apparently either don't know about these guidelines, or choose to ignore them.)

There is a new, well-maintained trail along the south bank of the upper river now, seldom used by hikers, almost never by fishermen. In many areas, it is much too high above the water to be of any use; but there are just as many places where it provides access to good spots that are very rarely fished, because they can't be reached from the road side. Just this past August, Pete and I had a fine afternoon and evening when we hiked the trail upstream from Apple Creek about two miles and then, wading wet, with the entire two miles to ourselves, worked our way back to where we had parked at the bridge.

The Camp Water may well be the best stretch of fly water on the North Umpqua; but the upper river is my favorite section, anyway.

Steelhead with fly

10

Heaven and Hell

*A foolish consistency
is the hobgoblin of little minds....*

EMERSON
"Self-Reliance"

IN A PLEASANT SHORT STORY by G. E. M. Skues, "Mr. Theodore Castwell,"
the title character, having died and been interviewed by St. Peter, is finally and
eternally stationed, with perfect tackle and an attending angel, on a beautiful
chalk stream with trout rising everywhere. Mr. Castwell hooks and lands one
two-and-a-half-pounder after another until, after hours of this all-too-

predictable success, he and the reader realize simultaneously that this isn't heaven, after all. It's hell.

It is worth summarizing the plot to make the point that if consistently good fishing is indeed hell, then the North Umpqua might be heaven—or at least something fairly close to it—because I doubt that there are many rivers anywhere as moody and unpredictable.

A simple comparison will help show what I mean. Many years ago, before the upper Klamath River steelhead fishing declined almost to the point of nonexistence, I fished there nearly every fall weekday morning between mid-October and Thanksgiving. Even these dates never varied by much: In the riffles I liked, between five and ten miles downstream from the old north-south highway, I never caught my first fish of the fall run earlier than October 12 or later than October 16; and in every year that I remember, the first big storm always swept in from the Pacific to put the river out of shape sometime in the last week of November.

I fished there only for five years, and five or six weeks isn't such a long season, so the predictability never seemed anything like hell to me—but predictable it was: Every morning I could be fairly certain I would catch two or three fish—rarely only one, never more than four, except on the occasional days when I put in extra time and raised the number of hooked fish proportionately. I could be just as sure that all of these steelhead would range between three and six pounds, the average size increasing slowly and surely as the season progressed. There were perhaps four or five I landed over the years smaller than three pounds, and only one bigger than six that I remember—a seven-pound female taken on Thanksgiving Day.

These were the same years that I was beginning to learn the North Umpqua, which is why the contrast remains so vividly in my mind. I never knew what to expect on the Umpqua, or when to expect it. The first sizable run of summer fish might arrive in the Steamboat area on June 10, or on July 10. When there were a lot of fish in the river, I might, on a rare and spectacular morning, hook six or eight or even ten big steelhead. Far more often, under what would appear to be identical conditions, I might fish hard for eight or ten hours, or even twelve or sixteen, with no time off even to eat lunch—fish with floating lines and sinking lines, with wet flies and dries, upstream and down, to the literal point of physical exhaustion—and never move a single fish.

It is something anyone hoping or planning to spend a lot of time on the North Umpqua had better get used to and adjust to: From one day to another, sometimes from one hour to the next, you rarely know what to expect.

The people who don't accept this heavenly state of affairs usually don't enjoy their North Umpqua fishing lives for long. When I worked at the inn I remember the arrival one August afternoon of a wealthy guest from a distant state, a handsome middle-aged man who was said to be an expert angler. As soon as he had his luggage in his cabin, he was back up in the dining room to ask about the fishing.

"There were a few hooked this morning," I told him.

"In the Camp Water?"

"There and downstream, too."

"Any big ones?"

"There've been some over ten."

"I'm going out right now."

"Now?" I asked him. It was at least ninety degrees and windy, about 2:00 p.m.

"Sure!" he answered. "Last August I got here in the afternoon and went right out and took two nice fish in the Station in fifteen minutes."

With that he was gone again—confident, exuberant—back down to his cabin to get ready to fish.

But he didn't hook any steelhead at the Station that afternoon; or anywhere else at the Camp Water, either, which he fished through the evening until dark.

We had a drink together after the dinner dishes had been cleared away and the other guests had gone down to their cabins to bed—it was his excellent bourbon, a brand I rarely had a chance to taste—and we talked about it.

"The mornings are usually better," I said, mostly because I believed it, but also because I considered it part of my job to offer encouragement. (And if we talked long enough, I might get a second drink of bourbon.)

"But last year I got two in the first fifteen minutes!" he told me for the sixth or eighth time.

"It was slow all over tonight", I said. "I didn't get anything downstream, or see anybody else with a fish on. None of the other guests did anything, either.

"But two in fifteen minutes! Right out there at the Station!" He wasn't merely troubled, he was angry at his blank afternoon and evening. He stared down at his glass on the big sugar-pine table and swirled the ice in it, eyes narrowed, tanned forehead deeply creased with a frown; and he left before I could finish my first-and-only drink.

This guest had been booked into the inn for a week, but two days later, almost exactly forty-eight hours after he'd arrived, and still fishless— strikeless, too, I believe—he finished his lunch, packed his bags, loaded up the big trunk of his expensive sedan and headed home in what had become a silent, fuming rage.

If it could have been arranged that afternoon, I'm sure he would have happily traded places with Mr. Theodore Castwell and gone to hell for some productive fishing.

Sometimes on the North Umpqua we think we know why things happen: A cloudy day after a long, hot spell in August—better yet, a cloudy day with a cool, light rain—will usually activate the fish; when the steelhead first arrive, or when they settle into new pools as the water drops, we can often raise them; when we are the first ones at a good place in the early morning, or first in the evening just after sunlight leaves the water, we fish, for good reason, with heightened expectations.

But most North Umpqua fishing is done in the summer and early fall, and most summer and early-fall fishing is done in places that have been receiving heavy pressure for weeks or months, on days that are warm and clear, and with only very minor fluctuations in the level or temperature of the water.

August is the month most typical of long hot spells and dour fish that, for days or weeks at a time, remain in the same holds and ignore, with apparent disdain, the dozens or hundreds of flies cast to them.

Once there were two steelhead, a male and a female, both ten-plus pounders, that moved into the Okie Pool at about the middle of August. They lay in plain sight over the gravel, the male five or six feet ahead of the female, reachable with a sixty-foot cast from the rock bluff at the head of the pool. (A few years later, the gravel washed out, so fish no longer hold there. Ever since the massive flood of December 1964, brought on by warm rains washing out a heavy snowpack, the river changes far more often and dramatically than it did in earlier years. It's even fair to say that to some degree the river must now be relearned every summer.)

I tried for that Okie Pool pair the first time I saw them, but neither showed the slightest interest in a fly. Probably because they were so easy to see, and their rises would be clearly visible if they ever did come up, I made it my routine to cover these fish every evening. The typical August weather never let up, and for ten days the two steelhead never moved. I tried big flies and small ones, bright and dark, wet and dry, but you might have thought they were glued to the bottom there.

On the eleventh day, everything seemed the same. I worked out about fifty feet of line and made a cast well short of the first lie because I wanted to soak the fly and make sure I was gauging the distance correctly. I was about ten feet short, as planned; but just as the Skunk began its slow swing, the male came quickly off the bottom in a surging rise. I saw the broad bright side as he turned, then the swirling boil on the calm surface. One second later, the rod was bowed against the weight of a running fish.

Eight or ten minutes later, I released him and watched as he disappeared down into the deep, dark water at the foot of the bluff.

Then I climbed back up to try for the female, but I really didn't believe I could be quite that lucky, which was why I didn't bother to retie. Of course she came up for the first cast, just as her mate had; and after three good jumps and a strong downstream run, the tippet snapped at the fly.

What had happened? Had anything changed? Nothing that I could perceive; but two steelhead that had never given any indication they even saw my flies chased them aggressively on the eleventh day.

During yet another August, Rob Carey and I fished for a few days out of the permanent camp I had set up on Frank Moore's land. We concentrated on the pools in that general area, and on our second morning I started off at Wright Creek. Things had been so slow up until then that we didn't get up until after seven, and Rob didn't even bother putting waders on. Instead, he sat on a comfortable rock high up the bank to watch. I hooked a good fish almost immediately. By the time he got his waders on, I had hooked and landed two more, and I was barely halfway down the pool.

We found willing steelhead everywhere we went that morning; and, most surprisingly, they kept coming up even after the bright, hot sun was on the water. The next day was the same. Then everything stopped again, as quickly and inexplicably as it had started.

It happens that way—not always, but often. In some months there will be three or four days—and not always consecutive days—when the fishing is unexplainably good.

On some otherwise slow days, it often happens that several people fishing widely separated pools all hook fish in a period of twenty minutes or half an hour; and not necessarily the first or last half hour of the day. It can happen at lunchtime, when only the hardest-working or most desperate fishermen are out.

In the middle of a summer with a high count of steelhead in the river, dozens of fish will normally be visible from the high banks in the well-known pools; but then they will disappear for days, and no one knows what happens to them. Maybe they go down into the deepest pools to be cool, or hold in the fast riffles for increased supplies of oxygen. But then, though nothing seems to have provoked it, they are suddenly back, holding in plain sight in the familiar places.

I've learned over the years that it doesn't usually pay to wait until you hear the fishing is good, because by the time you reach the river there's at least an even chance that it won't be good anymore. It makes at least as much sense to head for the North Umpqua when you hear that no one has caught anything for a week or more. When news like that gets around, the crowds will diminish; and by the time you arrive, there's a fair chance that things will have turned around, and you can enjoy the results on an uncrowded river.

Mr. Theodore Castwell will never know what he missed.

Col. Jim Hayden

11

The Gentleman and the Mechanic

*The man who cannot enjoy his leisure
is ignorant, though his degrees exhaust the alphabet, and
the man who does enjoy his leisure is to some extent educated,
though he has never seen the inside of a school.*

ALDO LEOPOLD
A Sand County Almanac

AN OLD AND DEEPLY VALUED family friend died not long ago.

Jack Decius began fishing the North Umpqua years before the paved road went in. He and his wife Anne were the Moores' first overnight guests after they bought the Steamboat Inn from Clarence Gordon. Hilde and I met Jack and Anne, and Jack's father Court, when we worked at the inn in the 1970s.

Jack was fifty years old then, and Court, who had introduced his son to fly fishing and the river, was over eighty — one of the fortunate few who knew the North Umpqua in the good old days back before the war. Court had been a very successful businessman in California, and Jack became a chemistry professor.

If I had to use one word to describe Jack as a person, it would be gentleman. He was always polite, always modest, always generous—traits which unfortunately seem to have gone decidedly out of fashion over much of the land.

I learned things about Jack at his memorial service in Corvallis that I'd had intimations about but had never really understood fully. He wasn't merely a connoisseur of classical music, he was a gifted cellist as well. He hadn't merely been accomplished in his academic field, he had been eminent. A book he wrote more than forty years ago—something well beyond my comprehension, about molecules in magnetic fields—is still highly respected and used today, a phenomenon virtually unheard of in the sciences. One of Jack's old colleagues told a revealing anecdote at the service.

"After I'd been at Oregon State a while I realized what kind of work Jack was doing and how respected he was. One day I asked him, 'Why do you stay here? You could go anywhere in the country. Anywhere in the world.' His answer was, 'I like the fishing.' "

Jack did indeed like the fishing. He truly loved it; and the one word which would best describe him as an angler is meticulous. He had something that went beyond patience. It was a serenity that I like to think related somehow to both his love of science and of fine music. I've fished with him, and watched him fish, in rainstorms and through long, hot days when no one was catching anything. No matter what the conditions or circumstances, he was always able to do what all of us should do but seldom manage: fish each and every cast as though this was the one that, if executed properly, would surely raise a fish. Jack was always happy fishing. The only thing that could break through that happiness was success, which made him ecstatic.

Hilde and I shared his fishing cabin with him the last year of his life, and I'll always remember the day he came back after raising six fish on one rainy early morning at the Station, one of his favorite pools; he was seventy-two years old and wore a smile as exuberant as that of any healthy youngster after the first good fish of his life.

I remember the way Jack laughed when he told me about the steelhead he caught on what may have been the driest fly ever. It happened when he was standing on a high rock at one of the downstream pools doing something with his reel, half his leader hanging from the rod, the fly three or four feet above the water, and an awfully aggressive steelhead jumped clear, hooked itself, and almost yanked the rod from his hands.

I remember how depressed he was after Anne died, and how he fought back and finally overcame it. He was a fine fisherman, a good man.

Many good men and women—and some not so good—have fished the North Umpqua over the years; and goodness, as it applies to rivers and fishing, has absolutely nothing to do with wealth or fame. Snobbish millionaires and so-called celebrities can be found in waders; but, except for the fact that they can sometimes get to distant and exclusive places where the fishing is probably too easy to mean much anyway, they have no advantages over the rest of us. True democracy can indeed be found on any public trout stream or steelhead river.

I never knew any of the true old-timers on the North Umpqua. Major Mott died before I was born, and Zane Grey, Fred Burnham, Zeke Allen, and Clarence Gordon were gone from the river long before I finally arrived, just short of my thirtieth birthday. By that time, men like Stan Knouse, Colonel Jim Hayden, and Court Decius had become the old-timers.

For years Stan tied the beautiful flies that Frank sold at the inn, and for a long time he held the unofficial record for the largest North Umpqua steelhead ever killed and weighed; a winter fish of over sixteen pounds. The pool that used to be known as the Upper Ledges—usually fished from the trail side—was renamed the Knouse Pool and marked with a plaque after he died.

To this day, there is an old trailer on Frank's land that used to belong to Colonel Hayden. The first time I ever saw the trailer, which was not a small one, it was parked between two of the cabins at the inn.

"What's in that thing?" I asked Frank.

"The colonel's booze."

"What?"

"That's how Colonel Jim carries his liquor and bar equipment around. That's why we have the mint patch out there behind the shed, too."

I would soon learn for myself that the colonel, a Southerner by birth, took his mint juleps just about as seriously as he did his steelhead fishing.

I met a lot of memorable characters in those days. Dee Avignon—soon to become "The Okie"—sauntered into the dining room one summer afternoon, took a seat at the sugar-pine table, and proudly announced, in an accent that seemed exaggerated even for a native of the state, that he was "the best fly fisherman in Oklahoma." After we saw him cast, we wondered if he was maybe the only one in Oklahoma; but he worked hard at it and learned, caught his share of fish, and he still comes back to Oregon every year to try, usually with good success, for steelhead and salmon.

Now that my son Pete is older than Hilde and I were when we began to fish the river, we've become—like it or not—a couple of the current old-timers, along with people like Joe Howell, Dan Callaghan, George Crandall, and others who began in the 1950s and 1960s. So it has gone, and will keep going, as long as there are rivers left to love with steelhead in them to fish for.

Now I want to tell about another fisherman, a young man I'll never forget, and whom I knew for only two weeks (his vacations, I assumed) of each of the first three summers I fished the river.

The strange thing was this: He couldn't cast forty feet. His tackle consisted of a beat-up fiberglass rod with the guides held in place by black electric tape, a rusty little reel that might have cost as much as two dollars sometime between the world wars, and a line so old that it appeared to be rotting away in places. His flies were ridiculous-looking creations, with the wings as likely as not to be tied on sideways or even upside down. He wore the latex rubber waders popular at the time (Seal Dris), but his were so old that they were made up more of many colored patches than of the original latex, and in them—despite the Korkers (metal-cleated wading sandals) he wore—he was so awkward that he tumbled off a ledge or rock into the river at least once every hour.

All he knew how to do was catch fish, and it was his example that made me believe irrevocably in the old theory that some people are born lucky and some people aren't. As far as steelhead fishing is concerned, I doubt that anyone was ever born luckier than this fellow.

Once, when I was fishing behind him in the Mott, I watched him make one of his typical thirty-foot casts, the fly landing well short of the roadside ledge. Even before he could begin to mend, a steelhead hit, then jumped and ran fifteen or twenty yards downstream, the old reel sounding like a sewing machine with two handsful of sand in the motor. The steelhead jumped again at the end of the run, and then the line went slack; he was off. So the fly began its swing. But before it was halfway across the run, another steelhead struck and was hooked. This one broke off after a couple of minutes, but it didn't matter much. Five minutes later, he hooked and landed yet another nice fish just downstream at the Glory Hole.

One evening as I walked down the trail from the ranger station parking lot, I saw him fishing the Sawtooth. Just as I was passing by, he tried to make what for him would have been a very long cast out into the deepest water. But he tried too hard, and it all fell apart; the line landed no more than fifteen feet away, in a hopeless mess of tangles and coils. I don't generally delight much in the misfortunes of others, but I stopped to watch, curious about how he would resolve his difficulties. After shaking the rod again and walking down the ledge and back up, nearly falling twice, he finally reeled the line tight. Of course, there was a good fish at the end of it—ten or eleven pounds—and he landed and released it.

On another evening that same year I was fishing the Station just after sunset, but I worked carefully all the way down through the pool with no sign of a fish. As I turned to wade back across, there he was, tall and gangly in his patched waders and floppy, black hat, soaking wet from having fallen in, but smiling happily.

"You going to try it?" I asked him.

"No, no!" he said. "I came over to tell you to fish the bottom end, way down. Sometimes they're holding down there this year. I've seen you out here before, and you didn't fish it far enough down. Right off that little rock"—he pointed with the old rod—"see where I mean?"

"Don't you want to try it?"

"No, no! You try it. Go ahead. I'll just watch."

He slipped and fell again, caught himself before he got wet, then sat on a rock to watch. On my second or third cast, I hooked a fish—exactly where he said I should.

I never even knew his name. I'm not sure anybody did. All we ever really talked about was fishing, because that was all we cared about on the river.

Both of us usually stayed at Island Campground, often with our tents in adjoining spaces. He drove a battered pickup truck before they became fashionable, and he seemed to live exclusively on tuna fish, whole-wheat bread, big green apples, and Blitz beer. I'm sure he wasn't formally educated, and his hands were deeply calloused, with signs of permanent grease around the nails, so I thought he might have been some kind of mechanic. One summer when the ignition on my little Toyota station wagon began to smoke and throw sparks, and show signs that it might explode or melt, he got his tools from the old truck and had it working perfectly again in minutes.

I still remember a conversation we had as we drank beers after fishing one night.

"Do you have any kids?" he asked me.

"Two," I said. "A boy and a girl."

"They old enough to fish yet?"

"My son's getting started on trout."

"I'm not married yet, but I'll have some kids someday. And they'll fish—you can bet on that. But you know what? The guys who were up here twenty, thirty years ago got the real fishing. They got the banquet, the big feast. We're getting the leftovers now. They're pretty good, the leftovers. I'm not complaining much. But our kids—they'll end up with the crumbs."

"I hope not."

"I hope not, too. But I think so."

After the summer of 1970, he never came back. It's possible he ended up in Vietnam; or he merely might have moved somewhere far away. That's what I hope, possibly north to Washington State—he mentioned the possibility once—and if that's what happened, I'm sure he's on another river somewhere up there now, perhaps with a son or a daughter, becoming an old-timer himself.

Whatever his fate, he's part of the North Umpqua, too, as surely as Zane Grey or Frank Moore or anybody else. Anyone who fishes a river for a single day, and truly loves it, becomes another living thread in that stream's life and history.

Frank Moore

12

Dynamite Works

The whole idea of fishing, it seemed to me,
was to hook a thrashing sea monster of some kind and
actually boat the bastard. And then eat it.

HUNTER S. THOMPSON
The Great Shark Hunt

STEELHEAD HOLDING POOLS along North Umpqua spawning tributaries, most often on Steamboat and Canton creeks, are dynamited with depressing regularity. Usually in August or September, with the streams at their lowest summer levels, a carload of crude, stupid men will sneak in late at night and slaughter dozens if not hundreds of steelhead at a time; and these are in a sense the most valuable fish of all, the ones that have made it safely in from the ocean and all the way upstream, through drift boats and bank fishermen, past night crawlers and gobs of salmon eggs, spinners and spoons, plugs and lures, and finally through the fly water, where many of them have been landed and released at least once.

I used to swim in some of the larger holding pools with my diving mask each summer, just to delight in seeing the big fish waiting there to spawn, but I almost always found something reprehensible: a shiny blasting cap wedged between rocks on the bottom or, hidden somewhere along the bank not far from the water, spears, nets or heavy lines with lead weights and big treble hooks for snagging.

In the summer of 1971 we caught two of these poachers as they drove down the Canton Creek road with their trunk full of freshly dynamited steelhead. There were between thirty and forty fish, I believe, and the two men who had done it were eventually convicted and fined about eighty dollars. I remember for sure that the fine came out to something around two dollars per fish. Though the penalties are considerably steeper these days, the dynamiting continues, along with all the other forms of poaching as well. (Just last March I was fishing the upper river when two young men from Fish and Wildlife stopped to talk. It turned out they were looking for two other young men who had been seen snagging steelhead on their spawning redds.)

A few years ago, my friend Rob Carey published a short story titled "Along the Umpqua," in which he compared and contrasted a fly fisherman and three dynamiters. The principal irony of the story is that these dynamiters talk about their "fishing" pretty much the same way fly anglers do: too damn many people are around these days; there sure aren't as many steelhead as there used to be; it's harder all the time to find a decent day of sport.

As far as these three are concerned, fly fishermen are contemptible snobs, and stupid snobs at that, because they don't have brains enough to kill their fish in the quickest, most efficient way. When you drive all the way to a river to get some steelhead, it makes perfect sense to get as many as you can—and nothing else does the job like dynamite. As an exercise in pure logic, it's hard to argue with that—unless you happen to agree with the idea that getting the greatest possible number of fish isn't really the point at all.

Not everyone will agree, but I believe the example of dynamiting is a fair way to introduce the subject of indicator fishing. To begin with, then, a quick definition: Indicator fishing as it's practiced on the North Umpqua fly water consists of using a floating line, a long leader, and a heavily weighted fly; often a very heavily weighted fly, sometimes a sparsely tied fly with less lead added. Several feet above the fly a strike indicator—a small, brightly colored plastic bubble, or a clearly visible hunk of yarn or wool—is fastened to the leader. This heavy fly, cast upstream, sinks very quickly, either reaching the bottom or coming near it, and if the indicator on the surface twitches or hesitates, even for an instant, the angler rears back and sets the hook. Often he sets it into a steelhead that has opened its mouth and perhaps moved a foot or two to quietly intercept the deep-running fly. Like dynamite (or spoons, spinners, plugs, lures, salmon eggs, worms), it works as a method of fishing.

My purpose certainly isn't to suggest that indicator fishermen are on a level with men who dynamite steelhead holding pools, or anywhere close to that; but it does seem to me that the whole ethical question of what works and whether or not we should do it simply because it works is at the heart of the current controversy over this increasingly popular form of fly angling.

Is it really fly angling, though? Old-timers on the river like Frank Moore, Joe Howell, George Crandall, Dan Callaghan, and many more, don't believe so. Frank calls the indicator people bait fishermen, or chuck-and-duckers. (If you've ever tried to cast a weighted fly you know what he means. When a hook wrapped with several layers of lead wire whistles past a few inches away from your ear, it makes you wish you were wearing a football helmet.)

It could be argued—has been argued—that these traditional anglers are merely jealous of a new and very effective technique; but it really isn't anywhere near as simple as that. Frank's counterargument is that the purpose of the original fly-only regulations passed back in 1951 was to protect fish. With runs dwindling even then, it was necessary to set aside several miles of river in which steelhead weren't very vulnerable, and the fly-fishing rule was an ideal way to do it. Frank and others knew very well that weighted flies fished deep were very effective any time of day, which was precisely why the new rules included a restriction against "all added weights and attachments."

Looking at it from this perspective, the problem is that indicator fishing clearly seems to be bending the original intent of the rules, and that it is indeed, in certain parts of the river, a very deadly way to catch steelhead. A deep-running fly can be drifted past a holding fish five or ten times, or ninety or a hundred times, if necessary. Sooner or later, when the fly comes close enough often enough, the fish will usually take it. It is even possible to hook the same steelhead many times in a single day, which never happens when the fish must be raised off the bottom to a fly on or near the surface. The argument here concerns whether or not a steelhead that is caught and released many times in a relatively brief period of time is likely to survive; and I don't believe anyone knows the answer to this yet.

On a personal level, I can report that there's really nothing new about indicator fishing. I taught myself to do it more than twenty-five years ago on the Applegate River (a major tributary of the Rogue). The Applegate is a winter stream, and all I owned was a floating line—I couldn't afford two fly lines at a time in those days—so, if I wanted to catch fish in January and February, I had to figure out a way to get the fly on or near the bottom.

I clamped a small split shot next to the head of the fly, ducked my head, cast well upstream, and worked my weighted Juicy Bugs back down through the runs and riffles. And I caught fish, many fish, sometimes behind men with bait and lures. I didn't use an actual indicator, but the

Applegate is a fairly small and placid stream, so the first few inches of my fly line served the purpose adequately. Whenever the tip of the line stopped, or hesitated, or moved in any unnatural way, I set the hook, usually into a good steelhead.

But as soon as I could afford a sinking line to take my flies partway down, I gave the method up. I liked the idea of raising a fish, even in winter. I wanted to really cast, not just chuck and duck. If I catch fewer fish now, I enjoy them more. This is especially true during the summer on the North Umpqua, where one of the strongest attractions is watching a steelhead's confident, surging rise through clear water up to the surface. I really can't imagine sacrificing such a sight; and another sacrifice the indicator fisherman makes is the sudden wrenching surface strike of a raised fish, surely one of the single most exciting moments in all of angling.

Considering all of this from a purely selfish viewpoint, I see no sense in giving up more than I can possibly gain. On a broader level, protecting fish should matter to us all.

Postscript:

The Station Pool is one of the most popular indicator spots on the river. Back before the road, when the ranger station was on the north bank near Steamboat Creek, it was sometimes called the Plank Pool, from the walkway of planks that Forest Service employees built from the bank out to the ledge on that side. These planks made it much easier to go out and get water, but they also made it much easier to go out and catch steelhead—too easy, as Frank Moore saw it. He believed the pool should be fished in the traditional way, which meant a long wade from the south bank all the way across the river, or a deep wade from the north bank.

Late one night he snuck down to the water and dismantled the walkway. "I was pretty worried," he says. "When I yanked those nails out, you could hear it echo all the way up and down the canyon." He finished the job safely, but some Forest Service employees soon rebuilt the walkway with heavier timbers and longer nails. So Frank snuck out again, ripped it out, and floated it down the river. They gave up after that, and no one called The Station the Plank Pool anymore. It has been fished the traditional way ever since—at least, until the advent of indicators.

Jack Hemingway fishing pool immediately above Steamboat Inn

13

In Fifty Years

*Conservation is a state of harmony
between man and land.*

ALDO LEOPOLD
A Sand County Almanac

NOT VERY LONG AGO, on a cloudy fall afternoon, along the upper river, I waded out to the edge of a slippery ledge which drops off to a deep channel dotted with jagged boulders. Though the boulders were twelve to fifteen feet down, I could see them clearly through the glassy water. Sometimes steelhead hold among those rocks, but not today.

About thirty feet across the channel is another ledge, and when I looked there I saw a good fish lying tight against it, near the bottom, straight across from me. It's always surprising to see them nosing into a current that way because they barely have to move to hold themselves steady. Every few seconds, the long steel-gray body will undulate. The tail might pump occasionally, but so gently that you have to look hard to see it happen.

I stood watching the steelhead, a nine-pound native male, and I knew it would take a good greased-line cast to get it. (I knew it was a native because I could see the adipose fin, which is clipped from hatchery fish.) I would have to curve my line in the air and drop the fly ten or twelve feet above the fish to drift it naturally down broadside in the current, directly ahead of the leader.

I worked out line in false casts until I thought I had enough, then tried it. The big Skunk dropped within a foot of where I aimed it and drifted down, the white wing spreading, moving in the current. When the fly was almost there, I looked back at the fish, just in time to see him rise.

When a steelhead comes off the bottom that way, in the right light something magical happens. The steelgray disappears, replaced by the rainbow colors. I saw the brown, black-speckled back, the red lateral line, the silver side, and snowy white belly. He rose quickly, but without apparent effort, as graceful as a soaring bird, growing larger as he came.

I saw the shiny pupil of his eye. Then his mouth opened wide and the fly was gone. He turned back down, as unconcerned and confident as when he had risen.

I set the hook, and the rod bowed into that sudden, heavy, wonderful resistance as the fish began his first powerful run.

My hope is that in fifty years someone, maybe my grandson Billy (though it's likely he'll be Bill or even William by then) will be out on that same ledge with another good steelhead in the pool, and the chance to experience what I have known; but if that is to happen, certain things will have to change.

The guiding principle behind true conservation is simple enough: We cannot take anything from the land—not trees, fish, water, or anything else—beyond a level that can be sustained in perpetuity for future generations. Despite the simplicity in this, efforts to save the North Umpqua River, or the Kalmiopsis Wilderness, or the very Earth itself, have become an incredibly complicated patchwork quilt of movements, protests, lawsuits, and perpetually shifting feuds and alliances among governmental agencies, business interests, and environmental groups.

It seems to me that the only thing that can possibly ever work on a large scale — really work, once and for all — is the general acceptance of the philosophy defined many years ago by Aldo Leopold in *A Sand County Almanac*: "We abuse land because we regard it as a commodity belonging to us. When we see land as a community to which we belong, we may begin to use it with love and respect. There is no other way for land to survive the impact of mechanized man..."

At present the health of the North Umpqua is most directly affected by mechanized man as represented by logging, dams, and fish hatcheries.

I'll always remember a large sign that had been erected beside the highway along the lower reaches of the fly water. Across the river was an area in which nearly all the mature trees had been blown down during the famous Columbus Day storm in 1962. The sign proudly proclaimed that the BLM had gone in after the storm and, in their own words, "planted a new crop of trees." Prudently, the sign was removed about ten years ago; and nowadays, thanks to new and more enlightened leadership, even government agencies are known to refer to vast stands of trees not as "crops," but as "forests."

As might be expected, timber companies have been slower to begin to come around. The September 1994 issue of *Timber Processing* magazine printed a sort of open letter from a man named Carl Jansen to workers in the "forest-products industry." Jansen wrote: "Almost all scientists agree that we are experiencing global warming due to increased amounts of carbon dioxide in the air... When wood is burned ... carbon dioxide is returned to the atmosphere... We in the timber industry are carbon stewards; we convert trees into building materials and other products that last a very, very long time. Have you ever considered the fact that by producing buildings or furniture we are actually keeping carbon dioxide out of the atmosphere?... In the U.S. and Canada we have built over 110 million housing units, amounting to an estimated 110 million tons of trapped carbon... In your conversations with people outside our industry, try to incorporate these issues in order to show how important our industry is to the global environmental picture."

This nonsense is on a level with the sworn statements of tobacco company executives who claim blandly that nicotine isn't addictive and that no one has really proved that smoking is harmful to health. It's beginning to seem at least possible that these greedy and desperate business people might eventually defeat themselves; that their blatant cynicism and hypocrisy is becoming so obvious, so absurd, that increasing numbers of people are seeing it for what it is and will act accordingly.

In 1938 Zane Grey sent a letter to the editor of the *Roseburg News-Review* to protest the netting of fish at the mouth of the North Umpqua, and the racks that were being used to trap steelhead upstream: "If properly protected," he wrote, "the Umpqua would want to be visited by every angler in the United States. There is no Canadian river that can compare with the Umpqua... As a matter of pure scientific fact, which any sincere naturalist will confirm, the salmon would multiply much more abundantly if left to propagate themselves. In the east, hatcheries have been found out to be merely rackets. I certainly hope Oregonians will wake up in time to save the Umpqua."

Zane Grey's sentiments remain very relevant today. It's possible that, even without a new and better philosophy regarding man's relationship with the land, Oregonians will wake up and decide to preserve the North Umpqua on purely economic grounds. It is one of the loveliest rivers on Earth and also one of the finest to fish, which makes it very rare and therefore very valuable: more valuable even than the trees along its banks or all the crops that its waters might be used to irrigate. And with a steadily increasing population of fishermen, it is worth more as a steelhead river all the time.

When I first read Grey's letter, I was surprised at what he wrote about hatcheries—that well over fifty years ago they were already seen as "rackets" back East. It wasn't until the 1970s that significant numbers of Westerners began to seriously question the effects of hatcheries on our salmon and steelhead rivers. Up until then, our coastal streams were widely regarded as convenient passageways where mass-produced smolts could travel to the ocean, feed and grow, and return eventually as mature fish. By now there are few—if any—honest biologists or knowledgeable fishermen who won't agree that hatchery fish are in every measurable way far inferior to native fish. Now the only serious argument made in favor of hatcheries is that they are a necessary last resort on unfortunate streams that have been degraded to a point where the rehabilitation of native fish populations has become impossible. The North Umpqua most definitely hasn't been degraded to that degree, and there are some hopeful signs for the future.

PacifiCorp is now in the process of applying for a renewal of its hydroelectric project at Soda Springs Dam above the North Umpqua fly water. Originally the utility proposed increasing hatchery production, but it has now agreed to consider spending its allotted $8 million on enhancing natural reproduction by either building a fish ladder over the dam to open spawning upstream or to improve downstream habitat. If the ladder is built, they will also install screens to keep young fish migrating downstream from washing into the turbines at the dam.

PacifiCorp has also agreed to control releases at the dam to avoid sudden drops in the water level, which can trap young fish in shallow pools and kill them. About a hundred miles south of the Umpqua, it actually looks as though authorities will soon remove Savage Rapids Dam from the Rogue River to cut down on the mortality of smolts moving downstream. If this happens, it could prove to be a very healthful precedent.

Over the past twenty years, with both hatchery and native steelhead in the river, North Umpqua summer runs have fluctuated from around three thousand to twenty thousand fish. Under sound management, an eventual stable population of between four and eight thousand native summer steelhead per year would probably be possible; and it would certainly be adequate, if aspiring anglers were willing to do just two things: learn to fish, and learn the river.

Of course there will be problems and controversies as far into the future as we can see, involving logging, dams, irrigation, pollution, and the varied and usually negative effects of too many people.

But I still want to believe we can make it work, that the North Umpqua, as well as other fine rivers that flow to the sea, will be seen right by enough people to make saving them possible; so I'm going to teach my grandson Billy to cast a fly, and I'm going to show him what I know about the river. That is one of my commitments to his future. I do want him out on that ledge, or on some other, in fifty years.